Barefooting

John Gillette's Complete Guide
To Barefoot Water Skiing

Second Edition

Copyright © 1987 by World Publications

All rights reserved. Reproduction or use, in any manner, without express written permission is prohibited.

Library of Congress Catalog Card Number: 80-53495
International Standard Book Number: 0-944406-00-9
Printed in U.S.A.

WE EAT, SLEEP,
RIDE, TALK,
BREATHE, LIVE,
& LOVE
BAREFOOTING

About The Author

The author and his wife enjoying one of their favorite pastimes.

John Gillette has been known around the world as "The Barefooter's Barefooter." He was instrumental in establishing and organizing the American Barefoot Club and has served as vice president, president, and chairman of the rules committee, as well as serving on the World Water Ski Union Barefoot Council.

A world class barefooter himself, John competed in international tournaments around the world, including two world championships. He also has a background in competitive water skiing and seven years of experience as a professional show skier. He has trained many of today's top barefooters and was the coach of the 1982 U.S. Barefoot Team. John's instructional articles have appeared in virtually every major water ski publication in the United States. His first edition of BAREFOOTING was published in 1980.

FEET TO FACE

Acknowledgements

I count it a privilege having had the opportunity to write this book, and it would not have been possible without the support of many people.

Terry Snow, Terry Temple and the staff of World Publications were the backbone of this project and made its publishing possible.

I greatly appreciate Tom King's outstanding photography which highlights the book and his sense of humor which kept us laughing during photo sessions. Also thanks to Dave Madeline, Paul Gerding, Harvey McLeod, Mike Botti, Correct Craft Inc., Barefoot International, AWSA and AWSEF for contributing photographs.

Leslie Dufka's artful eye is responsible for the attractive design of the book, and her wonderful personality made her a delight to work with.

I am grateful to champion barefooters Ron Scarpa, Mike Seipel, Rick and Lori Powell, Russ Conoley, Peter Fleck, Billy Nichols, and Mike Botti for sharing their valuable time, talent and techniques.

It has been only through the support and encouragement of my family that I reached a level of expertise enabling me to write this book. And I appreciate so much my wonderful wife Ann who patiently endured my long hours of work on this project, and whose love inspires me daily.

Above all, I acknowledge that except for God's unmerited lovingkindness and favor, none of this would have been possible.

Contents

Introduction **10**
History **12**
Equipment **22**
Safety **28**
Learning **32**
Start Methods **42**
Tricks **72**
Steering and Wake Slalom **100**
Jumping **110**
Endurance **116**
Rough Water **121**
Boat Driving **122**
Practice **126**
Competition **130**
Appendix **134**
Glossary **135**

Introduction

The challenge and thrill of skimming across the water at 30 to 40 mph on your bare feet while enveloped in a cloud of spray: It's a sport that's not for everybody. Not everybody has enough strength and coordination to be pulled successfully across the water on two small, naked pieces of flesh and bone. Not everybody has the courage to ski at such high speeds—much less without skis! Not everybody has a boat fast enough to even make an attempt at it. And not everybody has an instruction manual to tell them in detail all the steps necessary to make it possible.

Barefooting has been written as the manual for the sport. It provides a history of the sport and covers all aspects of the equipment necessary to become a barefooter. It teaches beginners the fundamentals and offers competitive barefooters up to date tips on the latest techniques. It also gives coaches, parents, and observers a basis for instruction to help aspiring barefooters. The information offered represents years of barefooting experience and success. When used properly *Barefooting* will quicken your skiers' progress and understanding of the exciting sport of barefoot water skiing.

The rapid development and refinement of barefooting skills have made it necessary to update *Barefooting* since its first printing in 1980. I have called upon the current leaders in the sport to assist in describing some of the latest techniques.

Mike Seipel, Ron Scarpa, Lori Powell, Rick Powell, and Russ Conoley are all national or world champions who are known for their skiing expertise and coaching abilities. This panel of experts represents a variety of barefooting styles and teaching techniques. For some of the maneuvers described, I have included several of these different ideas, recognizing that there is no one "right" technique for everyone. In some cases you may find one technique works best for your style and that another technique doesn't work at all.

This book should prove to be a valuable guide for every barefoot enthusiast. I trust that *Barefooting* will bring you to new heights of achievement and provide more enjoyment for every participant in this exciting sport.

HISTORY

Ever wonder what inspired the first barefooter to attempt such an unusual "feat?"

The first man reported to meet the challenge of barefoot skiing was Dick Pope, Jr. Back in 1947, Pope, who was an expert shoe skier, got to thinking one day: "If I can ski on skis barely larger than shoes, then why not ski with no skis at all?"

So he stepped off into the unknown. Pope's first attempts behind the boat in rough water were painfully unsuccessful. Still determined, he moved to calmer water and tried stepping off his skis while holding on to a training boom (a perpendicular bar) alongside the boat. On his second attempt, Pope became the pioneer barefoot water skier.

Three years later, the first barefoot competition was held at the 1950 Cypress Gardens Dixie Championships. Actually, the barefoot event would not have been held if not for an eager young skier from Mexico named Emilio Zamudio. Zamudio wanted to barefoot as his part in the trick competition. The judges, however, ruled that this was a ski tournament and the competitors must be on skis to be scored. Zamudio persisted and finally the judges were persuaded to hold a separate barefoot competition. Although Zamudio and Pope were the only two barefooters in the world at the time, other skiers quickly approved of the idea. They were eager to watch and learn — and to try barefooting themselves.

As the competition began, the first participants ended up with nothing but headaches until Dave Craig of Miami, Florida, successfully stepped off the ski on his second try. Then Stew McDonald of Tampa, Florida, managed a short ride without skis. Pope, unaccustomed to the rough water of the tournament area, had a difficult time but was able to move into first place with the longest ride. Finally Zamudio was up. He kicked off his ski, stood up

Ken Tibado innovated the "beach barefoot start" in 1955.

Dick Pope, Jr. was one of the first known barefooters.

HISTORY

high, and waved joyously at the crowd, winning the competition and shocking everyone with the apparent ease of his barefooting.

In 1955, the beach barefoot start was introduced. As the story goes, Ken Tibado of Lake Wales, Florida, heard that a group of Wisconsin barefooters had learned the beach barefoot start. The problem was, he had no idea of how to go about doing it. Determined not to be outdone, Tibado decided to try it himself.

His first thought was to stand near the water's edge with plenty of slack in the rope and have the boat take off at full speed. To succeed, though, the boat needed to be traveling better than 30 mph. After several attempts, Tibado concluded that this technique was only good for increasing the length of both of his arms!

Still determined, he developed another technique. This one involved a long running start, allowing sufficient distance for the boat to accelerate to barefoot speed before he reached the water's edge. What Tibado neglected to consider was that barefoot skiing speed is approximately 10 mph faster than any human has ever run. His attempt resulted in a painful, but spectacular, forward swan dive.

After careful analysis of the situation, Tibado reasoned that he needed more surface area to plane before the boat could reach enough speed to support him on just his bare feet. The most suitable planing surface for the job was his posterior. After sliding across the sand and into the water on his back, he could hold on long enough for the boat to reach speed and finally stand up. Many bruises and torn swim suits later, he perfected the technique. His surprise came when he learned that the Wisconsin barefooters had failed in all their attempts, making Tibado the first to succeed in beach barefoot starting.

Barefooting's first significant public exposure came at the 1956 National Ski Tournament in Laport, Indiana. A young skier named Mike Osborne approached tournament director Warren Witherell, who was unfamiliar with the technique and laughed in disbelief. But Osborne kept at him and Witherell finally decided to let him give it a try. That afternoon, Osborne thrilled the crowds with one of the first major barefoot exhibitions in the world.

Another unexpected barefoot demonstration turned up later in the same tournament in the mixed doubles competition. Tom and Jane Dorwin from Minocqua, Wisconsin, began with routine doubles maneuvers then suddenly stepped off their skis. The duo totally astonished the judges with the first double barefoot routine ever performed. Needless to say, with their spectacular performance the Dorwins easily won the competition.

In the years that followed, barefooters continued to become more and more innovative. Joe Cash jumped into the spotlight in 1958 with the first deepwater barefoot start, taking off in the water with no skis at all. His original starts were extremely demanding; he would sit doubled-up at the waist holding the tow rope handle near his feet. This method required a tremendous amount of strength and was soon phased out in favor of the much simpler technique of starting stretched out in a prone position.

The tumbleturn, one of the most popular barefoot tricks for the barefooter and spectator alike, began purely by accident. (To perform the trick, the barefooter falls onto his back and then swings his feet around in front to stand up again.) The trick was "invented" in 1960, when Don Thompson and Terry Vance were performing a double barefoot routine on the Lake of the Ozarks, Missouri. As Vance stepped off his skis, he began to fall. But while he continued to hang on, his feet spun around returning almost in front of him. Thompson (still on his skis) reached over and pulled Vance's legs around so that he could stand up. The next morning Vance tried repeating the maneuver. After a few falls, he perfected the trick for future shows.

Backward barefooting brought an entirely new dimension to the sport. Once again it was Dick Pope Jr. who attempted it first in 1950. But the whiplash on his first fall proved so painful that he vowed never to try it again.

It wasn't until 1961 that a person successfully barefooted backward. Randy Rabe of St. Petersburg, Florida started on a trick ski then turned around and planted his foot in the water while the boat accelerated to 40 mph, finally stepping off the ski. After enduring the pain and agony of countless falls, Rabe became very particular about who he would let see his technique. In fact, when he

In 1961 Randy Rabe became the world's first backward barefooter.

HISTORY

The early '60s saw Don Thompson appear as the first "superstar" of the sport, developing both back-to-front and front-to-back turnarounds.

demonstrated the act at Cypress Gardens, he allowed only the photographers in the boat.

The word soon spread that Rabe was backward barefooting, and Don Thompson became determined to learn the technique, too. His technique was to hold directly onto the boom along the side of the boat while riding a standard ski with the bindings turned around backward. With the support of the boom, Thompson made it on his second try, and within two weeks, was succeeding with every step-off attempt behind the boat. Realizing the show potential of the act, Cypress Gardens recruited him to ski in their show and to teach the other skiers the difficult maneuver.

A friendly rivalry developed between Thompson and Rabe who were both determined to learn new and different tricks. More often than not Rabe would be the first to try many of the tricks, but Thompson, the more experienced skier, would often be the first to succeed. For example, Rabe came up with the idea of barefooting with a girl on his shoulders, but Don was the first to be recorded doing it.

When Thompson began experimenting with the tandem barefoot idea, show director Dick Pope said it was too dangerous and would not allow him to practice it. Disregarding the warning, Thompson went out on the lake. Skiing on the boom along side the boat he held a 130 pound sandbag on his lap and then stepped off. Finding no problem, he tried it again with the sandbag on his shoulders. Then, with still no problem, he successfully substituted young Davey Holt for the sand. Confronted with these successful attempts, Pope conceded and Don Thompson and Jolene Nathy made barefooting history with the first tandem barefoot ride in a show.

Thompson started the back-to-front turnaround and the front-to-back turnaround in the Cypress Gardens show in 1962. Being the only skier in the show capable of backward barefooting, he performed it in four shows a day, seven days a week. At the end of each ride, he would attempt a turnaround. In took awhile, but the odds stayed with him, and eventually he became proficient at these turns too.

Meanwhile, barefooting interest was taking hold on the other side of the world. In 1960, an Australian barefoot water ski club was established. In 1963, they held a National Championship which

Participants in the 1973 Cypress Gardens Barefoot Championships. From left to right: tournament director Pat Callan, chief judge Stew McDonald, Mike Botti, Grant Torrens, Chas St. Cyr, Jenny Davis, Garry Barton, Bill Price, Mary MacMillan, Peter Trimm, John Gillette, Rudy Stout and John Hacker.

Barefooting 17

HISTORY

Brett Wing was unbeatable, winning the first three consecutive world championships.

was the first step toward barefoot tournaments as we know them today.

This organized competition began breeding excellent barefooters. By 1970, the Australians had gained a "foothold" on the sport and were beginning to show the Americans a trick of two. Barefooter extraordinaire Garry Barton began to tap the potential of the sport by introducing many new tricks such as the back-to-front step-over. Garry also designed today's barefoot handle that permits recovery from a toe-hold position in order to attempt the reverse toe-hold.

In 1973, Cypress Gardens invited the Australians up for an international competition. Garry Barton, Peter Trimm, John Hacker, Grant Torrens, and Mary McMillan, Australia's best barefooters, accepted the invitation. As expected, they astonished everyone and made a clean sweep of the tournament. Not one Australian came close to being beaten by a Yank. In fact, grandmother Mary McMillan out-footed some of the American men! Still, they brought a wealth of knowledge to the United States.

As late as 1976, barefoot competition in the United States was limited to a small group of enthusiasts. Then in the summer of 1977, John and Margaret Hacker returned to the United States and began to stimulate an interest in the sport. By instructing and demonstrating the advanced techniques of barefooting and by promoting the first world barefoot tournament scheduled for the following year (1978), the Hackers spurred the development of the American Barefoot Club (ABC).

Within one year, the ABC sanctioned regional tournaments and held the first National Barefoot Championships in Waco, Texas. Randy Filter of Muskego, Wisconsin, won the men's overall title, while Jean Matthisen of Hartland, Wisconsin, captured the women's overall title. However, show skier Mike Botti (Sea World of Ohio) had the most outstanding performances, placing first in start methods, wake crossing, and tricks. Because Botti elected not to enter the jump event, under World rules he was ineligible for the overall title.

Following the National tournament, Randy Filter, Mike Botti, Mike Seipel, William Farrell, Rob Beman, John Gillette, and Jean Matthisen were selected to represent the United States at the World Barefoot Championships and became the first official U.S. National Barefoot Team.

In 1986 this strong United States Barefoot Team finally toppled Australia's dominance of the World Championships. From left to right: Jennifer Calleri, Don Mixon, Jr., Mike Seipel, Ron Scarpa, Punky Forgiana, Russ Conoley, Lori Powell, John Cornish (coach), Rick Powell, William Farrell, John Strasser, James Baron (trainer) and Stew McDonald (manager).

HISTORY

In November 1978, barefooting history was made in Canberra, Australia, where 54 barefooters representing 10 different countries gathered on the banks of the Molongo River for the long awaited first World Barefoot Championships. As expected, the Australian team made a clean sweep of every event in both men's and women's divisions. Aussies Brett Wing and Colleen Wilkinson captured the men's and women's overall honors.

New Zealand and the United States were neck and neck for the runner-up spot. But the Yanks' mere one year of tournament experience showed through as the Kiwis skied consistently and squeaked by for the second place medal ahead of the U.S. Following were Belgium, The Netherlands, France, Austria, Germany, and Italy, respectively.

The Australians had proved their dominance of the sport. But during the finals, Mike Botti showed the potential threat of a strong U.S. team by placing third in tricks and fourth in jumping. (It was the first time he had ever jumped too!) In addition, he was the first to complete a wake front-to-back and wake back-to-front in competition. Knowing that the Americans had less than a year of competitive experience under their belts, the Aussies left the tournament wondering what they would have to contend with at the next world tournament.

Three more world tournaments came and went (1980 San Francisco, 1982 Acapulco, and 1984 Australia) and Australia held on to the team overall title, although with three-time World Overall Champion Brett Wing in retirement, U.S.A.'s Mike Seipel finished as the men's overall champion in 1984. It was at the 1986 World Championships in West Germany that the U.S.A. finally captured the team overall title.

As the sport continues to grow, many new and amazing tricks are constantly being developed; toe-hold turns, step-overs, wake turns, one-foot turns, 540's and more have been accomplished. "What else is there you ask?" The answer is left only to the imagination and determination of the young competitors in this progressive and challenging sport.

"Banana" George Blair has promoted the development and popularity of barefooting through his generous financial contributions to the sport and his intriguing and popular personality.

Mike Seipel grabbed hold of the world overall title after Brett Wing retired.

Stew McDonald has advanced barefooting, beginning as a participant in the 1950s and progressing to become an official and administrator through the 1980s.

EQUIPMENT

The Boat

Any boat can be used for barefooting as long as it is fast enough. However, there are certain boat characteristics that will make barefooting easier and more enjoyable. The best size boat is between 16 and 20 feet in length. Any smaller, the boat will probably be too lightweight, allowing the skier to pull it around. A larger boat sacrifices maneuverability and may throw an uncomfortably large wake.

It is commonly thought that the boat needs to be lightning quick out-of-the-hole for barefooting. This is not true. In fact, too much acceleration is usually worse than too little. However, the boat should not be sluggish to the point that it takes excessive energy for the skier to get up and go.

Another major consideration is hull design, which affects the turbulence of the wake. On flat bottom boats the propeller is closer to the surface, causing more turbulence than a deep-V design. (NOTE: If the wake is excessively turbulent, experiment with lengthening the rope to find smoother water.) The flat bottom also tends to produce a larger stern roller which can make deepwater starts more difficult.

Proper trimming of an outboard or stern drive can be very helpful for barefooters. Trimming-in the engine will keep the bow low when planing off, thereby increasing acceleration and reducing the size of the stern rollers. Once on plane, the trimmed-in engine will aim the propeller thrust deeper into the water and reduce wake turbulence. Trimming-out the engine is useful if more top end speed is needed. This raises the bow, reducing the wetted surface of the boat, and less drag means more speed.

The premier barefoot towboat in the world, Correct Craft's Barefoot Nautique.

Handles

There are many different types of handles used for the various barefoot maneuvers. These will be discussed with their respective uses later in the book.

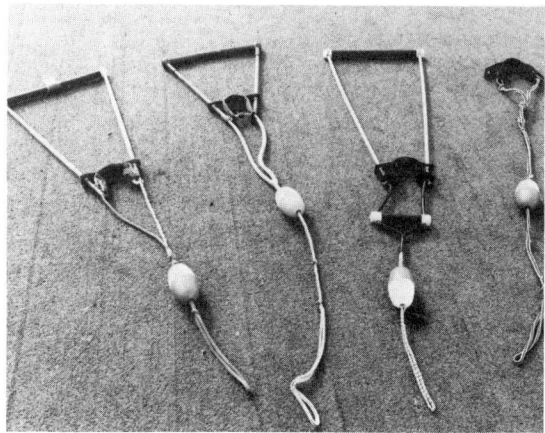

From left to right: longer forward toehold handle with teeth strap, forward toehold handle with beartrap, backward toehold with spreader bar and toe start strap.

Ropes

Minimum stretch is the primary consideration when choosing a good barefoot rope. The common polypropylene line has a high elasticity which is undesirable for barefooting. Polyethylene rope is best for barefooting. Although it stretches when new, soon it will become "stretched out" and lose its elasticity. A 1/4" or 5/16" polyethylene rope is preferred by many barefooters.

When barefooting inside the wake, the best rope length will vary depending upon the turbulence, boat speed and the maneuver you are attempting. Generally a 100 foot line will place you far enough back to have calm water inside the wake. If the turbulence is particularly bad, you may want a longer rope. However, the longer the rope the more stretch

EQUIPMENT

it will have. Also, extra long ropes can have a sag problem which decreases the solidity of the pull.

When barefooting outside the wake, there are two factors that will affect how long the rope should be: The spray from the boat, and the trough or gully next to the wake. You should be back just far enough so neither factor adversely affects your skiing. Generally 75 to 85 feet is sufficient.

In competition a 75' line is used in wake slalom and jumping, and in start methods and tricks either a 75' or 85' line is provided. In tricks it is also permissible to bring a line of your own preferred dimensions and material.

Three versions of step-off skis, from top to bottom: longer jump ski style backward step-off ski, forward step-off ski, shorter trick ski style backward step-off ski.

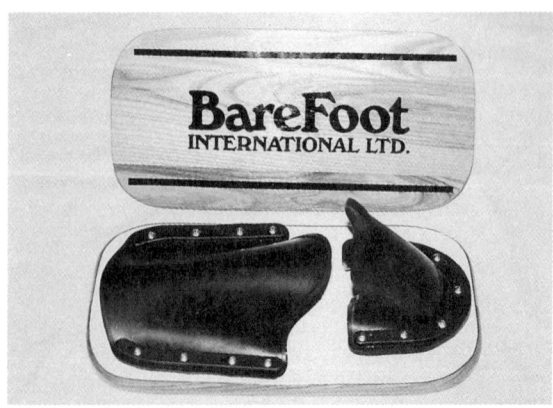

Small shoe skis like these can be excellent learning aids for various tricks.

Skis

Any ski can be used for a forward step-off. However, competitive slalom skis with lots of rocker should be avoided because they tend to jump off the water when you step-off. (The high cost of slalom skis also may give you second thoughts about leaving your ski floating out in the lake.) It is best to step-off of a conventional flat bottom ski.

You never know when you will get tangled up with the ski during a fall. Because of this, the ski should be free of any sharp or hazardous edges.

Back barefoot skis (see page 52) can range in size from shoe skis to surfboards. Still a conventional flat bottom ski is fine, although some people prefer the stability of the larger jump ski. Generally the bindings should be placed close together and positioned near the center of the ski. Heel pieces are generally not used.

Wetsuits

The minimum equipment a barefooter should wear is a safety jacket and watertight shorts. The watertight shorts can be anything from overlapping pairs of tight cut-offs to elaborate padded rubber shorts with adjustable leg straps. A wetsuit of some type is recommended for many tricks and starts which require sitting or lying on the water. A sturdy short-sleeve or full-length suit will often suffice. However, the specialty barefoot wetsuit is a necessity for any serious barefooter.

A barefoot wetsuit prevents an unexpected enema caused by sitting on the water. It also provides flotation, which is usually built into the wetsuit and this makes the wetsuit a substitute for a ski jacket or life vest. A barefooter's wetsuit provides a smooth surface for the body to glide across the water during start methods and tumbleturns. It pads the body from the force of the water, particularly during start methods and tumbleturns. And finally, it is built to endure the rigors of barefooting.

Refinements of the barefoot suit in recent years have resulted in a suit of thinner neoprene rubber, with padding added to areas that need it. Most barefoot suits come in a thickness of three to four millimeters, although a thinner two millimeters or less is available from some manufacturers. The thinner material is more flexible, which allows for easier movement and better fit. This thinner material, however, provides less padding.

The primary places a barefooter needs padding are in the seat (which contacts the surface of the water frequently), and on the back and chest (for tumbleturns and backward deepwater starts).

Generally, a double layer of neoprene rubber is sufficient padding in the seat, while layers of ensolite (material used for flotation) pad the back and chest.

Recently, some manufacturers have added a reinforced crotch to wetsuits. This padding does have some value in routine barefoot activity but certainly doesn't replace an athletic cup for men performing deepwater back starts.

The need for padding in the arms is minimal, while the need for freedom of movement is great. Therefore, many barefooters prefer extremely thin and flexible neoprene in the sleeves, or short sleeves, or even no sleeves at all. The best style for you will depend on your climate (long sleeves if it's cold), the amount of protection you desire, and what is most comfortable to you. Not all sleeveless suits work well. During tumbleturns or recoveries from a fall, a sleeveless shoulder can catch water easily, quickly applying the brakes.

The legs on a barefoot suit need to be long enough so that the water will not catch the edge of the wetsuit when you're sitting or lying on the water during a deepwater start. Full-length legs can cause problems by catching the spray from your feet and they can get bunched up easily above the calf during falls. Therefore, they should only be used when Mother Nature makes it necessary.

Standard-sized suits work well for most people, but if you aren't standard size and shape, remember that many manufacturers offer custom-fitted and even custom-designed suits for those who like to foot in fashion. Prices range from $150.00 to $350.00.

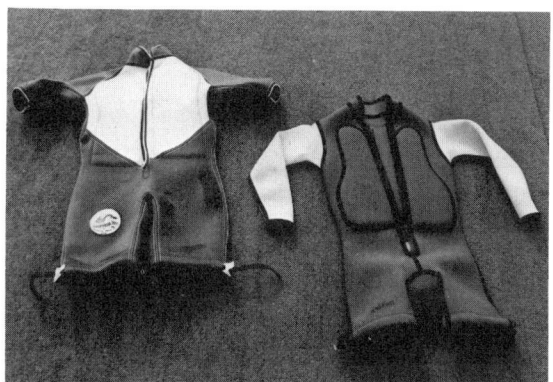

Short sleeve (left) and long sleeve (right) barefoot wetsuits with built in padding and leg straps.

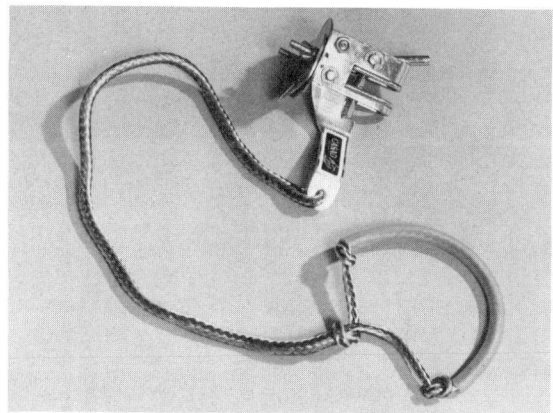

The safety release.

Safety Release

The safety release is a safety device designed to release the rope from the boat in case the ski gets caught in it. It is primarily used when the skier is holding with his foot, teeth or neck. Because of the quickness of barefoot falls, the release is only as good as the person who operates it. Ultimately, it is the skier's responsibility to get out of a bad situation without a release. Do not rely on a release. Use it only as a back-up.

The Barefoot Boom

The boom or "training bar" as it is sometimes called, is a metal pole protruding 5 to 10 feet from the side of a boat. A skier may ski on a short 5 to 10 foot rope attached to the boom, or he may hold directly onto the boom using it as a ski handle. Most barefoot start methods and tricks are easier to learn on it. However, some things can be more diffi-

EQUIPMENT

cult on the boom because a short rope sometimes gives the skier a pendulum or swaying effect.

There are three reasons why barefooting on the boom is easier. First, it gives the skier a straight pull through calm water. To receive the same smooth water behind the boat, the skier would have to be outside the wake. Having to cut or "hold an edge" to stay outside the wake often makes tricks more difficult.

Secondly, using a short rope on the boom gives the skier an upward lift. This upward lift is especially helpful when learning tumbleturns, because it lifts your shoulders off the water, reducing drag. Less drag makes the spin of the tumbleturn easier. On start methods, the upward pull helps lift you out of deepwater and onto your feet during the stand up.

Thirdly, holding directly onto the boom gives exceptional stability for beginning barefooters. This has proved to be an almost sure-fire way to teach even the most inexperienced skiers.

In addition to making the skiing easier, the boom also makes the instructing easier. With the skier just a few feet away from the boat, the instructor can better observe his movements.

Since barefooting on the boom is easier, it may make barefooting behind the boat seem more difficult. Therefore learning things on the boom is fine, but once they're learned they should be practiced behind the boat.

Not all boats are suitable for booms. Light boats will be pulled around considerably by a footer on the boom, making steering dangerously difficult for the driver. Boats equipped with a boom should weigh at least 1500 pounds (including motor and equipment). Inboard tournament boats are generally heavy enough and stable enough for the use of a boom.

Shorter booms are stronger and exert less leverage on the boat, therefore affecting the boat's handling less than longer booms. However, the boom should be long enough to keep you a safe distance away from the boat and away from any of the boat's spray. (Once while doing a tumbleturn on a short boom I ended up hitting my head on the side of the boat!)

CAUTION:
Barefoot booms can be dangerous. Only experienced skiers and drivers should use them. Carefully follow the instructions provided with each boom.

All cable connectors and stress points should be inspected frequently. Serious injury could result to skiers or passengers in the boat if something were to break, allowing the boom to swing across the boat.

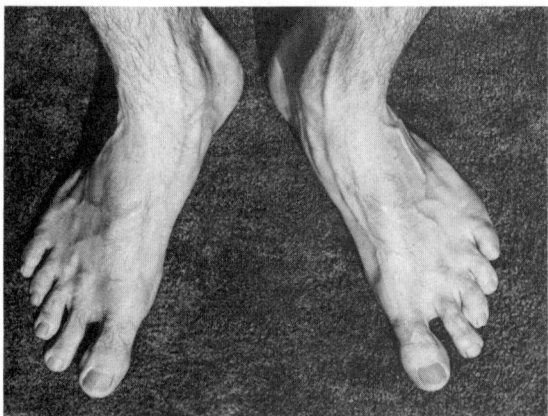

Your most important equipment.

26 Barefooting   *The barefoot boom or "training bar."*

SAFETY

Learning To Fall

There is no denying that barefoot falls are often hard and painful. The high speeds required cause falls to come quickly and sometimes catch you completely off guard. You must learn to fall correctly to minimize the risk of injury. The best thing you can do when you fall forward is to tuck your head and roll over a shoulder. After a while this should become an automatic reflex to you. If it doesn't, give this book to someone else and find another sport.

Some of the worst falls of barefooting are caused by holding on to the handle a moment too long after catching a toe. This will prevent you from tucking and will lay you out into a hard face-first SLAM that will roll your eyelids back. Let go of the rope as soon as you fall forward!

On the other hand, as long as your feet are out in front of you, you can usually pull out of a potential fall. If you bounce back onto your derriere, hold your breath, hang on, and rock forward on to your feet.

THE IMPROPER TECHNIQUE FOR FALLING.

Barefoot falls are often hard and painful.

SAFETY

Barefooter's Signals

The following are common skier/driver signals:

1. Faster or increase speed: Shake head or handle up and down, or thumb pointed up.
2. Slower or decrease speed: Shake head from side to side, or thumb pointed down.
3. I'm all right: Fallen skier should clasp both hands overhead to indicate he is okay.
4. Turn: Circular wave of the arms or hand in the direction of the turn.
5. Rough water ahead: Wavy motion of hand.
6. Smooth water ahead: Slicing motion with flat palm downward.
7. Take off: Loud and distinct "hit it."

Falls like these are why toe straps that don't come off during a fall can be dangerous.

Safety Do's And Don'ts

Adhere to the following do's and don'ts for the safe enjoyment of barefooting:

- Do wear a snug-fitting life jacket; A loose vest can be dangerous.
- Do wear watertight shorts to prevent intrusion of water into unwanted places (traumatic enema).
- Do check your step-off skis for sharp or protruding objects that can snag or cut your skin.
- Do learn new tricks progressively, working up to your skill level.
- Do signal driver "I'm all right" after a fall by clasping both hands overhead.
- Do have a competent driver who understands the signals and is familiar with the driving needs of barefooters.
- Do keep track of dropped skis so you won't barefoot over them; pick up your skis as soon as possible.

30 Barefooting

Holding the handle too long during a fall will prevent you from tucking and make the fall more dangerous (above and left).

Releasing the handle quickly, tucking your head and rolling forward is the best way to fall when you catch a toe.

- Do make your signals clear to the driver; a mumbled "no" or "wow" can be misinterpreted as go. Use the verbally distinct "hit it" to signal your start.
- Do be cautious of getting tangled in the ski line; people have lost fingers, toes, and received nasty rope burns.
- Do use common sense; think things through before doing them.
- Don't yell "hit it" until the line is tight and your body is in the proper position.
- Don't put any part of your body through the handle bridle (only experienced barefooters should attempt the rope on neck and rope in teeth tricks mentioned later in the book, even then I don't recommend them).
- Don't put the rope between your legs.
- Don't barefoot in shallow water; minimum safe depth is five feet.
- Don't attempt fast landing toward shore; let go far enough from the shoreline so you sink into four or five feet of water.
- Don't barefoot in unfamiliar water.
- Don't barefoot in water with floating debris. (I once barefooted over a dead catfish. It took pliers to pull the barb out of my foot!)
- When double barefooting, don't continue to barefoot if the other person falls. (I once was tripped up and dragged by a loose rope.)
- Don't use a stretchy ski line; the handle can slingshot into your legs or feet.
- Don't use a boom unless it is properly constructed and safely installed.
- Don't attempt to hang on and "tumble-out" of a face-first fall. This can lead to serious injury.

Barefooting 31

LEARNING

With a strong desire, just about anyone can learn to barefoot. However, before attempting to barefoot you should be very comfortable on one ski and in pretty good physical shape. Some individuals have learned without any previous water skiing experience, but this is the rare exception. Also, to ensure maximum success and safety, choose perfectly calm water.

There are three ways to learn barefooting: the step-off; the kneeboard start; and the boom start. If a kneeboard or a boom is available, use them; they are generally easier methods of learning. All three will be discussed in this chapter.

One Ski Step-Off

Land practice is very important when learning the step-off. Tie a handle with at least five feet of line to a solid object. With the handle in hand and the rope tight, assume a position as if you were skiing on one ski. Then crouch down and set your rear foot about two feet to the side and 12 inches in front of your ski foot (the foot that would be on the front of the ski), as if you were putting it in the water. This foot should be banked or angled at about 20 degrees with the toes up. Concentrate on the following key elements of the pre-step-off position:
1. Knees bent
2. Three quarters of your weight on the bare foot
3. Bare foot banked and ahead of the ski foot
4. Bare foot leg slightly straighter than ski leg
5. Handle at waist level
6. Arms bent
7. Shoulders slightly behind hips
8. Feet shoulder-width apart

While in this position, practice the motion of dropping the ski and planting the other foot. There will be a moment where most of your weight is supported by your bare foot with the rest "suspended" in the air. It is during this quick moment that you have to transfer your foot from the ski to the water. This is difficult to simulate on the land because the ski will not slide on solid ground like it will on the water. However, by rocking all your weight onto your bare foot you can practice the motion of shoving the ski to the side and reaching the forward barefoot position.

Now get the feel of the barefoot position. Everything is the same as the pre-step-off position except that your feet are about a shoulder-width apart with weight distributed evenly between them. Visualizing the correct pre-step-off and barefoot positions before ever attempting them on the water will prevent many unnecessary falls.

Land practice is important when learning the step-off.

LEARNING

Before you try the step-off on the water, you will need to decide where you want to do it: Inside the wake, outside the right wake or outside the left wake. If the water is very calm outside, that is probably the best choice. The ski should be kicked away from the wake. So if you are planting your right foot, stay on the left side of the wake. If you are planting your left foot, be on the right side of the wake. Do not drift too far away from the wake because the farther away you are from the center of the wake, the more awkward the step-off will be.

If your boat has very little turbulence or if the water is rough, you might be better off inside the wake. Avoid the turbulence directly in the center of the wake. Position yourself in an area of smooth water between the turbulence in the middle and the wake on either side.

Out on the water, move yourself to your selected spot inside or outside the wake and signal the driver to accelerate to your barefoot speed.

Get into the pre-step-off position by gently placing the heel of your bare foot on the water beside

The side view sequence shows proper positioning of the foot and the "sitting-in-a-chair" position.

Keep your arms slightly bent and handle near waist level. Gently place your heel on the water.

Begin applying weight to the foot while gradually pressing it out in front of you.

34 Barefooting

the ski. Begin applying weight to the foot while gradually pressing it out in front of you until you reach the pre-step-off position as practiced on land: Knees bent, three-quarters of your weight on the bare foot, bare foot banked and ahead of ski foot, ski leg bent more than bare foot leg, handle at waist level, arms bent, shoulders slightly behind hips. If you are properly positioned, there will be a lot of spray coming off the foot.

If you find it difficult to plant your foot at barefoot speed, slow the boat down 5-8 mph to where the water will be softer and easier to set your foot in. Replant your foot and have the driver speed up to normal barefoot speed. As the speed builds, gradually apply more weight to the foot.

When you are ready to drop the ski, give it a shove to the outside while momentarily rocking more weight to your bare foot. Step to a shoulder-width stance, applying even pressure to both feet. Keep your arms in, weight back and toes up. If the maneuver is executed properly, you will probably get some spray in your face.

Shove the ski to the outside while momentarily rocking more weight to your barefoot.

Step to a shoulder width stance, applying even pressure to both feet.

Barefooting 35

LEARNING

Do not jump off the ski. Step off smoothly and gently. The only part of your body that should significantly move is your ski leg. Everything else remains unchanged from the pre-step-off position. It is crucial to have a good pre-step-off position to have a successful step-off.

The step-off is much easier if your foot is not in a binding. Even a toe piece makes it more difficult. Either take the binders off completely or set your foot on top of the binding.

Problem/Diagnosis

Problem: *Catching toes while planting foot.*
Diagnosis: *1. Foot is too level. 2. Foot is underneath you too much. Push it out in front more. 3. Not enough speed. 4. Water is too rough.*
Problem: *Foot skips or hops off the water when trying to plant it.*
Diagnosis: *1. Foot has too much angle. Bring it underneath you or lower the front of your foot slightly (the foot should be approximately 90 degrees to the lower leg.) 2. Bend your bare foot leg knee more.*
Problem: *Does not feel like you can drop the ski.*
Diagnosis: *1. Not enough weight on your bare foot. 2. Wrong pre-step-off position.*
Problem: *Catching a toe when stepping off.*
Diagnosis: *1. Too much body movement. 2. Not enough speed. 3. Placing second foot on the water too flat or underneath you too much. 4. Poor pre-step-off position.*
Problem: *Getting pulled over forward.*
Diagnosis: *1. Arms are outstretched. 2. Legs too straight.*
Problem: *Falling shortly after stepping off.*
Diagnosis: *1. Standing up too straight. 2. Too far forward. 3. Feet are not banked enough. 4. Water is too rough - try it another day.*

Standing up too high makes you prone to catching a toe.

Arms outstretched and bent over at the waist is less stable.

36 Barefooting

Kneeboard Start

The first challenge in learning to barefoot from a kneeboard is getting up on the board in a sitting position. Have the driver take the slack out of the line and keep the line tight. Straddle the middle of the board like sitting on a horse. Signal the driver to accelerate slowly to 10-12 mph. Lean back against the pull, raising the nose of the board above the water like a ski. At the same time, place your feet out in front of you above the water.

Once you are planing and stable you need to move your weight forward on the board to keep it from bouncing. To do this, place your feet on the nose of the board. Put one hand on the board behind you, but keep the handle centered with the arm bent so that you do not get turned sideways. Now slide your buttocks forward as far as possible by supporting your weight with your feet and hands. Once this is accomplished, grab the handle with both hands and take your feet off the board.

ddle the board in the water.

Lean back as the boat begins to pull.

Shift your body weight forward on the board.

tly set your heels in the water.

Transfer more weight to your feet as the boat accelerates.

The board will fall behind, leaving you on your feet!

Barefooting 37

LEARNING

Prepare to stand up by bending your arms and knees and holding the handle at waist level. When you are ready, place your heels in the water with your feet almost level. This is the signal for the driver to begin accelerating to barefoot speed. As the speed increases, apply more and more weight to your feet, and increase the angle of your feet by *slightly* straightening your knees. You will encounter a lot of spray if properly applying weight, so hold your breath! As barefoot speed is reached, simply rise off the board by rocking forward and straightening your knees more (like getting out of a chair) and the board will drop behind you.

Be sure to remember these basics: Arms bent, handle at waist level, shoulders behind hips, knees bent, and feet banked.

Problem/Diagnosis
Problem: *Board bounces radically up and down.*
Diagnosis: *1. Too far back on board. 2. Going too fast.*
Problem: *Catching toes when planting feet.*
Diagnosis: *Feet too level and/or applying too much weight too soon. Increasing the speed to around 20 mph before planting the feet may help.*
Problem: *Cannot stand up off board.*
Diagnosis: *1. Leaning too far back. Bend forward slightly placing your weight over your feet. 2. Not enough speed.*
Problem: *Pulled over forward when standing up.*
Diagnosis: *1. Arms outstretched. 2. Legs straight.*
Problem: *Catching toes when standing up.*
Diagnosis: *1. Feet too level. 2. Not enough speed.*

Begin on your stomach.

Roll to your side.

Boom Start

Attempting the kneeboard start while holding directly onto the boom is the easiest method of all for learning to barefoot.

Learning to barefoot on the boom without skis or a kneeboard is a somewhat unorthodox technique but often the most successful method. It is strongly recommended that you use a wetsuit to provide padding for the stomach, hips and thighs.

Grip the boom a safe distance away from the boat, and have the driver accelerate to 3 to 5 mph slower than your normal barefoot speed (see page 40.) As the boat reaches barefoot speed, turn your hips and legs sideways and tuck them up close to your body. Take as much of your weight as you can in your arms and swing your feet around in front of you. With your body squarely facing forward, gently place your feet on the water about shoulder width apart with knees bent. If your knees are straight, your feet will dig in hard and catapult you forward. Transfer the support of your weight from the boom to your feet, keeping them out in front of you. You're barefootin'!

Problem/Diagnosis

Problem: *Can't swing feet around in front of you.*
Diagnosis: *1. Not tucked up enough. 2. Not lifting enough weight with your arms. (It is almost like a chin up.)*
Problem: *Toes constantly catch when placing your feet on the water or putting weight on them.*
Diagnosis: *1. Setting feet on the water too level. 2. Knees bent too much. 3. Feet not in front of you enough. 4. Not enough boat speed.*

If your feet do catch and drop behind, hang on anyway. You can catch your weight with your arms and try it again without having to stop the boat.

Tuck your legs up and lift them in front of you.

Plant your feet and stand up!

Barefooting 39

LEARNING

Foot Position

Part of developing the feel of barefooting is understanding the use of ankle and foot positioning. This comes naturally for many people, but some people need to make a conscious action to obtain the correct positioning.

Generally the best angle of attack, or "bank" as I frequently refer to it, is between 10 and 20 degrees. A steeper angle of 30 degrees may be necessary for rough water or slow speed.

The foot is usually kept at a 90 degree angle to the lower leg, although pointing the foot (plantarflexion) may be necessary when first setting the foot on the water prior to standing up from a sitting position. Planting the foot with too much angle will cause it to skip, rather than plane smoothly on the surface.

Pulling the front of the foot up toward the shin (dorsiflexion) may be necessary in rough water or when standing up very high in calm water. It takes practice to develop the feel for good foot positioning.

To summarize, a sharply banked foot keeps the toes high off the water so they are less likely to catch, but it also is more tiring and may drown you in spray. A foot with very little angle planes smoothly with little spray, but makes you susceptible to catching a toe.

How Much Speed?

Being as close to water skiing and barefooting as I am, I take it for granted that people know what speed is required to ski barefoot. One day, I was walking back from lunch with Tiella Parrish, a new show skier at Sea World who was recruited from somewhere in Missouri. As I learned, one thing they don't know in Missouri is how fast is fast; all they know is you have to go fast—but not how fast.

To my amazement, Tiella explained to me that until she ran across my first book on barefooting, she had tried a few step-offs at breakneck 55 mph, not realizing that 35 mph was more than enough for her. As you can imagine, a few falls at that speed quickly discouraged her from further attempts.

So Tiella made me realize that barefooting is still unfamiliar enough to the public that some people don't yet know how fast they need to go. If you fit that category, here are some guidelines for you. And even if you're already a barefooter, you might discover some insight into your own specific speed requirements.

Weight is the primary consideration in determining barefoot speed. There have been formulas that theoretically calculate your speed from just your body weight. The traditional formula is to divide your weight by 10, then add 20. For example, my 140 pounds (where's the beef?) divided by 10 is 14. Add that to 20, and I get 34 miles per hour—which works out pretty well for me.

No formula, however, can accurately predict speed for everybody, because foot size and shape also make a difference. A lightweight skier may have very small feet, requiring him or her to go faster than a heavy person with banana boats for feet. Also, a flat foot will require less speed than a highly arched one, as will a wide foot.

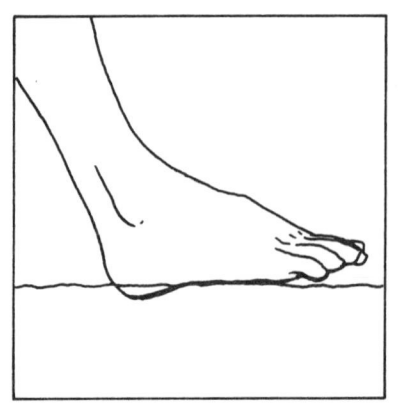

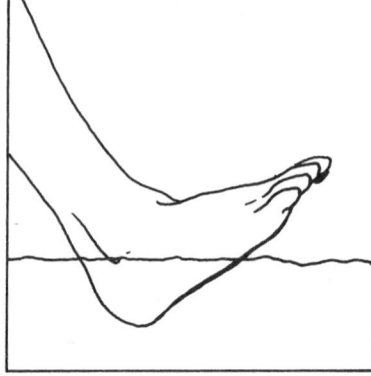

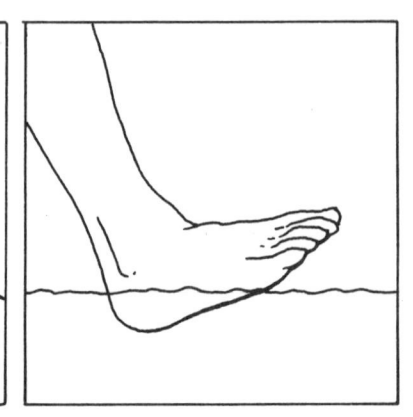

Too flat.   *Too banked.*   *Just right!*

A prime example of this is big Bob Baker, a 200 pound human piece of steel who is very comfortable barefooting at 35 miles per hour on his size 12s. On the other hand, dainty 110 pound Debbie Connoyer (formerly Debbie Berndt, the first United States female back barefooter), with her petite 6 1/2s, requires almost the same speed as Bob to barefoot comfortably.

So, there are no hard-and-fast formulas for determining your best barefooting speed, only rough indicators. The only way to know is to feel the water underneath your feet. If you have the correct barefooting position, the water should be breaking about in the middle of the arches of your feet. If just your heels are in the water, you're going excessively fast. If the water is breaking near the ball of your foot, more speed is required.

The accompanying chart provides approximate forward two-foot speeds for you. These are not minimum barefoot speeds, but those that are recommended for comfortable forward footing.

WEIGHT/FOOT SIZE/SPEED CHART

Foot Size	Under 100 lbs.	100-140 lbs.	140-180 lbs.	Over 180 lbs.
Small	34 mph	36 mph	38 mph	40 mph
Medium	31 mph	33 mph	36 mph	38 mph
Large	28 mph	30 mph	34 mph	36 mph

Many barefooters feel they need more speed than they actually do. This often results from poor body position, such as leaning too far back with your feet plowing the water too far in front of the rest of the body. If you do this, you may sense that your feet are deep in the water. It is your body and foot position or inexperience, though, that is causing this sensation, not your speed.

The advent of the one-foot forward wake slalom demonstrates how slowly barefooters can go. Due to the wake characteristics of some boats, the maximum speed possible before hitting the rooster tail is 38 to 39 mph. Therefore, even husky guys like Ron Scarpa and Mike Seipel are performing forward one-foot wake slalom at this relatively slow speed—a notable accomplishment. And remember, they're not just standing there on one foot. They're cutting back and forth across the wake, sometimes in rough water. So, if 170 pound Ron Scarpa, with average size feet, can do that at 38 miles per hour, certainly a smaller barefooter can find support on two feet with considerably less speed.

Backward barefooting requires even less speed than forward barefooting. This is because the front half of the foot (that is the section in the water) is much wider than the heel. The toes provide planing surface as well, and the water can rise quite a way up the heel before causing the foot to trip. So generally, you can knock off about two miles per hour from your front barefooting speed for the backward barefoot.

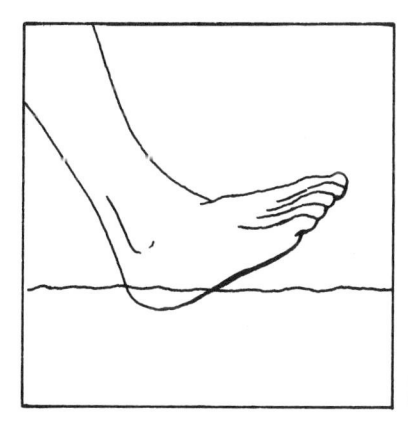

Too fast—less stability and harder falls.

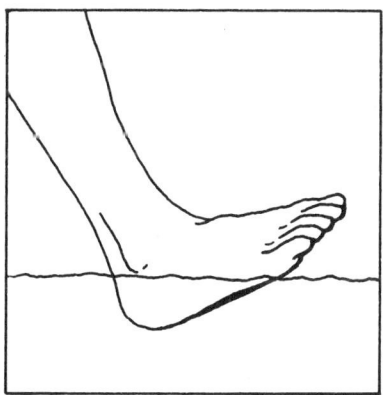

Too slow—foot is deep in the water, susceptible to catching a toe.

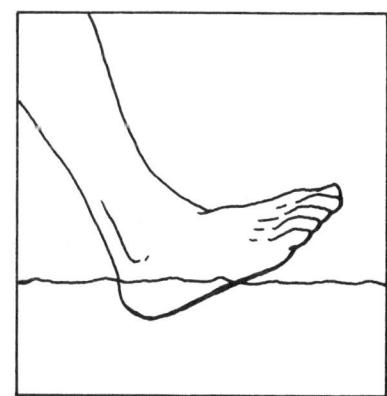

Just right!

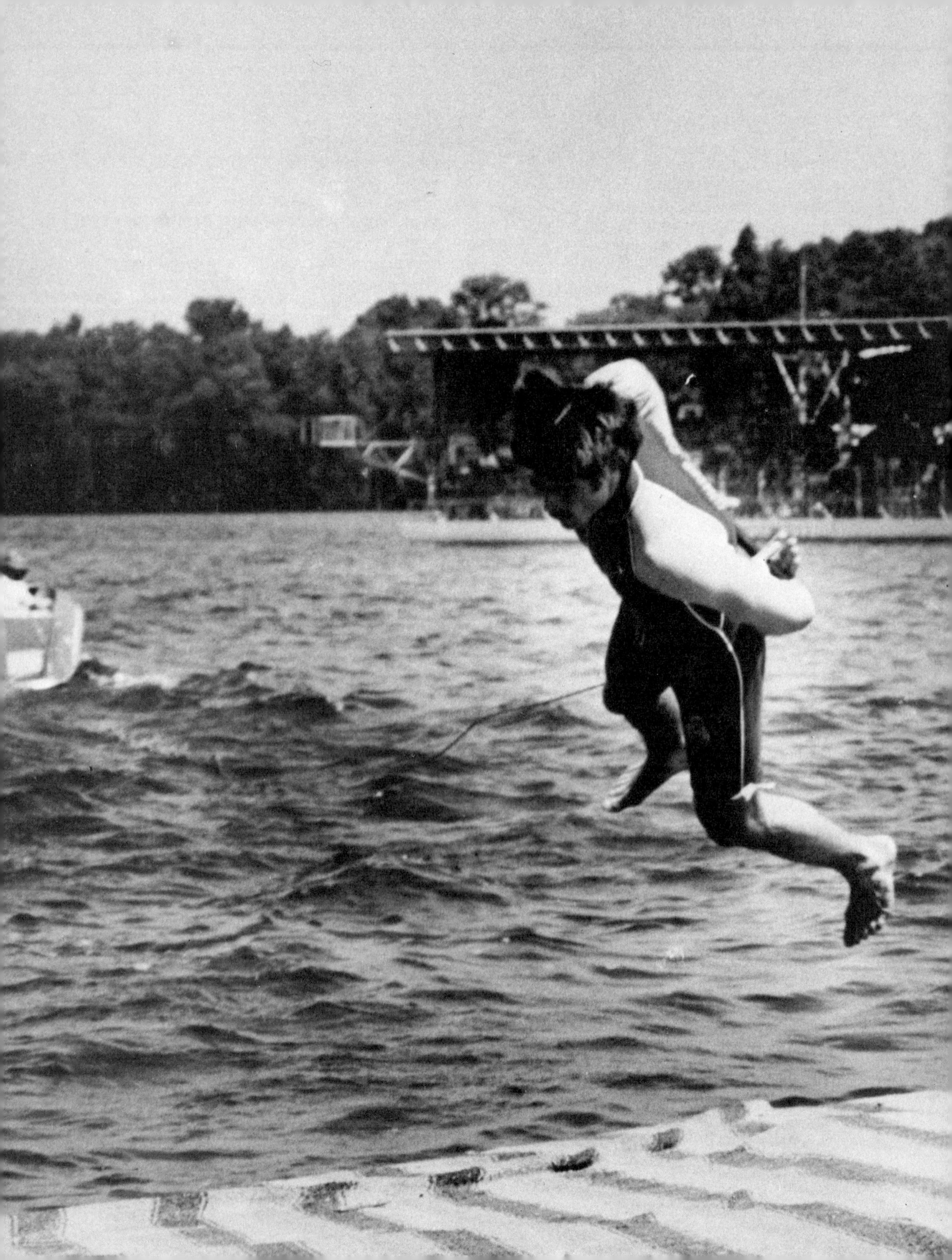

START METHODS

Once a person has mastered the art of skiing on his bare feet, his next challenge will be to attempt a new start method. Spectators are thrilled at the sight of a ski-less person sliding across the beach and barefooting away (beach barefoot start). In fact, the beach barefoot start or a variation of it is so exciting it is traditionally found in almost every water ski show. It is a great feeling when you reach the point where you can abandon the step-off ski and need only a boat and tow rope. Practically every conceivable start has been accomplished by barefooters, including the flying backward toe-hold start, the backward toe-hold jump-out, and believe it or not, Australian Garry Barton has even completed a rope-in-teeth deepwater start!

A Word To The Wise

It is true that it only takes a boat and tow rope to accomplish many of the starts covered in this chapter, however, unless you enjoy pain, here are a few tips that make the starts easier, safer and more enjoyable.

1. Wear a wetsuit or watertight shorts. Almost all the starts involve sitting or laying on the water, so you should have a layer of protection between you and the water.

2. Use a shorter handle. Eleven inches is good for first attempts. It is easier to hit your feet or legs with a longer handle when you have to abort beach, deepwater and flying starts. Also, be sure to spread your feet and legs before releasing the handle on any fouled starts.

3. Always use flotation for safety and comfort. Flotation built into a wetsuit is recommended. If a ski vest is worn externally, tighten the bottom strap as tightly as possible to prevent it from catching water.

4. Males should use an athletic cup when learning backward deepwater starts. (Guys have used everything from ski binders to kitchen towels to provide personal protection.)

The Deepwater Start

There are four steps in a deepwater start:
1. Getting set in the water.
2. Planing off.
3. Riding up to barefoot speed.
4. Standing up

Begin a deepwater start in the water, lying on your back with your feet toward the boat. Hold the handle near your waist and keep the line taut (photo 1.) Place one foot on the line for stability and to prevent you from being pulled over the front. Place the arch of your foot on the rope and point your foot in at about a 45 degree angle.

Instruct the driver to keep the boat moving forward as slowly as possible—with just enough speed to keep the line taut while you get ready. If you're being pulled too fast, you will be unstable and find yourself gasping for air. When you're ready, yell "hit it". During the hesitation, place your other foot on the rope, arch your back by throwing your head back as far as possible, and press down on the rope with your feet, having instructed the driver to hesitate for two or three seconds before acceleration (photo 2.)

The key to proper deepwater starts is arching your back by throwing your head back and keeping your feet low or on the rope. In this position, the arch of your body will act like a trim tab on the back of a boat, and the flow of water against your back will lift you to the surface.

You may sometimes have a tendency to roll over before planing off. To prevent this, hold the handle with both palms facing down. This keeps the shoulders and torso square. Put one foot on the line and use your free leg for balance. You can compensate for any rolling by raising or lowering your free leg. I didn't realize until writing this that I have unconsciously used only one leg on the line all the time. When I put both feet on the line (the traditional procedure) for the photos, I found it less stable.

Many people are under the impression that you

1979 National Starts Methods champion Rob Beman performs a flying backward dock start.

START METHODS

need a quick yank out of the water to execute the deepwater start. This is entirely false. While it is true that some tow boats need a wide-open throttle plus a few paddles and kicks to pull someone up, today's high-horsepower boats, full-throttle, out-of-the-hole acceleration can make a start more difficult as well as more hazardous. Moderate acceleration via progressive application of the throttle is best.

After you feel yourself plane off and the water becomes firm, bend forward into a sitting position (photo 4.) If you bend forward too soon, your butt may dig into the water and your feet may rise, resulting in excessive water pressure and the handle being pulled out of your hands. Keeping your body arched too long can make you bounce. Experience will help you to determine the proper time to bend forward.

You can ride for a long time in this stable sitting position with your feet on the rope, so don't rush putting your feet in! Wait until barefoot speed is reached. Rushing the stand-up is a common beginner's problem.

If you are unstable or begin bouncing during the sitting stage, take your feet off the line and place them lightly on the water. This will give you good stability. However, be careful not to put too much weight on them until you reach barefooting speed, or you may catch a toe.

Once you reach barefoot speed, lift your feet off the line by leaning back slightly and bending your knees. You should also continue to keep the handle low and arms bent. Outstretched arms reduce control and tend to pull you forward.

Gently set your feet on the water with knees bent, and transfer weight to them by rocking your body forward and straightening your legs slightly (photo 5.) Planting your feet with too much vertical angle will cause them to jab hard into the water rather than plane smoothly. This can also be caused by planting your feet with legs straight. When this happens, think about pointing your feet downward, in a "planter flexion" as podiatrists say, to make your feet more parallel with the surface of the water. This movement comes naturally for most people, but some need to make a conscious effort to accomplish it (see page 40.)

One last note on the forward deepwater start: It is the best start in barefooting for getting water up the nose. Your nose is in the perfect position to act as a scoop. Although this is generally just a nuisance, there are times when the water pressure is so great that it will actually make your ears hurt. In fact, one friend of mine spent the night in the hospital after he almost blew his eardrums out! Use caution if you develop excessive pressure in the ears. The best solution to this problem is a nose clip. Some people blow air through their nose during the start. I just endure it and avoid doing too many deepwater starts.

Hold the handle near your waist and place one foot on the rope for stability.

Arch your back by throwing your head back and keeping your feet low on the rope.

The flow of water against your back will lift you to the surface.

Problem/Diagnosis

Problem: *Instead of rising and planing on the surface, you go down and rake the bottom like a drag line.*
Diagnosis: *1. Not arching your back far enough. Make sure your arms are bent, with your head arched back as far as possible, and you have a slight downward pressure on the rope with your feet.*

Problem: *Rolling over prior to reaching a plane.*
Diagnosis: *1. Arching before the boat begins to pull. 2. Legs not bent evenly; it might help to keep one foot off the rope to use for balance right up to the point of standing up.*

Problem: *Feet fly up and your rear digs in.*
Diagnosis: *1. Not enough arch. 2. You bent forward before sufficient speed was reached to support you on only your rear. 3. Not pressing down on the rope with your feet.*

Problem: *Bouncing when traveling across the water.*
Diagnosis: *1. Not putting enough weight on the rope. 2. Too much acceleration. 3. Leaning back too far. 4. Rough water.*

Problem: *Can't get a plant.*
Diagnosis: *1. Legs too straight. 2. Feet are banked too much. Make your feet more level to the water.*

Problem: *Can't stand up.*
Diagnosis: *1. Not enough speed. 2. Not rocking forward enough. 3. Legs too straight.*

Problem: *Pulled over forward.*
Diagnosis: *1. Arms outstretched. 2. Legs too straight. 3. Not enough speed. 4. You're rushing it. Do it slowly!*

Problem: *Uncontrolled stand-up.*
Diagnosis: *1. Feet too close together. 2. Legs straight. 3. Leaning back too far. 4. You're rushing it. Do it slowly!*

Feet On The Rope Vs. Feet Off

"To keep them on, or not to keep them on, that is the question." Keeping your feet on the rope, that is. Every forward barefoot beach, deepwater, or dock start performer must make this decision. Once planed off, some footers ride all the way up to barefoot speed with their feet on the rope, while others place them on the water right after planing off. What's the difference?

In calm water with a stable ride, keeping your feet on the rope provides stability and control. It also means less fatigue and less spray. If, however, you hit some waves or find you are losing control, placing your feet lightly on the water about shoulder width apart with knees bent will provide lateral stability until enough speed is attained to stand completely on your feet. Caution must be taken not to place too much weight on your feet too soon, though.

Either way is acceptable and works well. You should let what feels good to you and the water conditions help decide which style to use.

After planing off, bend forward into a sitting position.

Gently set your feet on the water with knees bent.

Stand up by rocking your weight forward and slightly straightening your legs.

START METHODS

The Beach Barefoot Start

Select a smooth or grassy beach with a gentle slope toward the water. Sit about twenty feet from the water's edge (farther if your boat has slow acceleration). Have the driver idle out to stretch the line tight, then place your feet on the rope with your legs almost straight. Your feet should be pigeon-toed at about a 45 degree angle so that the arches of your feet are on the rope with your feet slightly crossed. Begin in a sitting-up position and remain in this position throughout the start. Some people have the misconception that they need to arch their backs when taking off the beach. This is dangerous.

Feet on the rope provide less fatigue and spray.

Feet off the rope provide more stability in rough water.

When you are ready, signal the boat to go. You should be going about 15 mph when you hit the water. Maintain a slight downward pressure on the line with your feet for stability (but not so much that your feet go under the water). As you slide into the water, you will be supported by your butt and thighs. From this point you continue just like a deepwater start.

The beach barefoot starting position.

Problem/Diagnosis

Problem: *Legs fly up, butt goes down when taking off from the beach.*
Diagnosis: *1. Leaning back too far and not putting enough pressure on the rope with your feet. Rock your weight forward slightly. 2. Not enough speed when you hit the water.*
Problem: *Bouncing when traveling across the water.*
Diagnosis: *1. Not putting enough weight on the rope. 2. Too much acceleration. 3. Leaning back too far. 4. Rough water.*
Problem: *Can't stand up.*
Diagnosis: *1. Not enough speed. 2. Not rocking forward enough. 3. Legs too straight.*
Problem: *Pulled over forward.*
Diagnosis: *1. Arms outstretched. 2. Legs too straight. 3. Not enough speed. 4. You're rushing it. Do it slowly!*
Problem: *Uncontrolled stand-up.*
Diagnosis: *1. Feet too close together. 2. Legs straight. 3. Leaning back too far. 4. You're rushing it. Do it slowly!*

The Dock Start

The dock start is essentially a glorified deepwater start. All you do is jump in and do a deepwater start. You can either stand on the edge and jump in or take a running start.

I recommend taking a few steps to get some forward speed so that you don't have any chance of hitting your head on the dock. Standing on the edge and jumping may result in your head coming dangerously close to the dock.

You can also avoid this danger by jumping off the side of the dock parallel to the direction you will be going. This isn't nearly as spectacular, though, as running and jumping, but it is safer.

Select a dock that is low and long enough to provide you with three or four running steps. The water should also be a minimum of five feet deep. Stand three or four steps from the edge of the dock with the boat stationary and the line taut. Signal the driver to begin a fast idle (5-8 mph.) Allow the boat to pull you to the end of the dock, rather than running faster than the boat which creates slack rope. When you reach the end of the dock, push off and kick your feet out in front of you so that you land on your back. You can hit the water in an arched position as in a deepwater start, in a straight position with no arch, or even in somewhat of a pike position. The important thing is to arch immediately after you hit the water. Otherwise, your feet may be forced up and the pull of the rope will cause you to buckle forward at the waist. As in the deepwater start, remember to arch by throwing your head back while keeping your feet low, near the rope.

Although landing in an arched position will reduce the possibility of buckling, it will also painfully smack your back. For that reason I suggest landing in a slightly piked position so that you land butt-first. Arch as soon as your butt hits the water. From this point, continue your deepwater start. You can either leave your feet off the line or place them on the line as you arch (see page 45 .) Do not attempt to place your feet on the line while you're in the air; there is no tension on the line to support your feet.

Instruct the driver to hesitate a second or two before accelerating after you land. Better too little acceleration than too much, particularly in the learning stages.

Depending on the power of the boat and your ability, it is possible for the driver to provide full power from the very beginning, without any hesitation when you hit the water. You can gradually increase the acceleration each time you do the start.

Take a few steps to get some forward speed.

Push off and kick your feet out in front of you so that you land on your back.

Arch your back immediately after you hit the water.

Barefooting 47

START METHODS

Two Ski Jump-Out

The two ski jump-out, seen in many ski shows across the country, is one of the more spectacular barefoot starts. Yet it is one of the simplest to perform. Jumping out is easiest if your feet are not in the bindings (or no bindings are on the ski), although skiing at 35-40 mph without bindings is no piece of cake. Depending on the skis and your ability, you might find it best to obtain more control by having either your heels in just a heel piece or your toes very lightly in a toe piece.

You'll need fairly firm water for this start, so 2-4 mph faster than your normal barefoot speed is good (see chart on page 41.)

Your best bet is to attempt the jump-out in very smooth water outside the wake. Begin in a crouch position with your arms bent and handle held at waist level. When you build up enough nerve, make a slight hop straight up, kicking the skis behind you and to the outside. Concentrate on keeping your torso erect and landing directly on your feet without leaning back too far. Many people have a tendency to land with their legs too straight and feet too far out in front of them. For a good feet-to-feet jump-out you need to land with your feet underneath you—not way out in front of you. Additionally, you must land gently by using your knees as shock absorbers, letting them bend upon impact. If you land properly, the height of your jump won't matter.

To make the start more consistent, in rough water, sit down on the water as you land, allowing your bottom to take some of the weight. You should still land feet first though—feet then butt!

Problem/Diagnosis

Problem: *Feet dig in and cause you to catapult out the front.*
Diagnosis: *1. Landing stiff-legged and not absorbing shock with knees. 2. Arms are outstretched.*
Problem: *Landing hard on buttocks and bouncing forward.*
Diagnosis: *1. Leaning too far back in the air; keep your torso erect. 2. Feet too far out in front of you.*

Begin in a crouch position with your arms bent and handle at waist level.

Make a slight hop straight up, kicking the skis behind you.

48 Barefooting

Forward One-Foot Stand-Up

To receive credit for a one-foot start in competition, the foot to be held in the air cannot touch either the water or the rope.

The one-foot stand-up can be initiated from a beach, flying, or deepwater takeoff. Unless the water is very smooth inside, it is best to move outside the wake. After the initial acceleration, have the boat level off at around 25 mph Then, while sitting on the water, "cheek it" outside the wake by turning and banking your "cheeks" (buttocks, that is) to steer across the wake. Get a good cut at it, building enough momentum to carry you outside the wake. This is fun in itself!

Once you cross the wake, find a stable place to ride in the trough and signal the driver to accelerate to barefoot speed. When the speed is reached and you are stable, lean back slightly, lifting your foot off the rope. With your knee very bent (skiing leg), set your stand-up foot just above the water directly in front of you and close to your buttocks. Then in one motion, rock forward and stand straight up on the foot. The key is to plant your foot close to your body with your knee extremely bent. Rock forward and stand straight up.

The one-foot stand up can be practiced by repeatedly standing up and sitting back down on the water to attempt it again without ever having to slow the boat. However, after sitting on the water at 40 plus mph several times, you may develop a case of the hot seat!

Problem/Diagnosis

Problem: *Foot skips when trying to plant it.*
Diagnosis: *You are planting your foot too far out in front of you. Bring it in closer by bending your knee more.*
Problem: *Cannot seem to stand up on the foot.*
Diagnosis: *1. You are not rocking forward enough. 2. You do not have enough speed.*
Problem: *You fall over to one side when standing.*
Diagnosis: *You are not planting your foot directly in front of you.*

Keep your torso erect and land directly on your feet.

Land gently, using your knees as shock absorbers.

START METHODS

Place your stand-up foot directly in front of you with knee bent.

Rock forward and stand straight up on the foot.

Tumbleturn Start

The tumbleturn can be either a start method or a trick performed once up on your bare feet. It requires a bit of strength in the arms, but with proper technique it can be performed by any size barefooter of either sex. In fact, experience shows women usually have the smoothest technique because they do not have the greater strength to rely on.

The boom is a great aid for learning tumbleturns. When using a five-foot bridle on the boom, your arms and shoulders are lifted upward, reducing your body's drag on the water. The reduced drag requires less effort on the start and helps keep your shoulders from catching the water.

Begin by planing on your stomach. If you have a problem breaking the surface, experiment with different body positions until you find the right combination for you. It helps to keep your head and the handle above the water with your arms bent, using your forearms as skis. Be sure to hold the handle with both palms facing down.

For stability, as you begin planing continue to ride on your forearms by digging your elbows into the water. A slight downward pressure with your knees will also keep you traveling in a straight line and reduce any tendency to bounce around. Maintain this position until you pass the stern rollers.

When the speed is at least 20 mph, roll over onto your back, being sure to tuck your head and curl your shoulders to reduce the possibility of digging them into the water. If you find yourself bouncing on your back, try spreading your feet and pressing your heels gently into the water. Bouncing also can be controlled by riding slightly tilted (about 30 degrees) to one side with the elbow and leg on the low side pressed into the water.

Some skiers prefer to tumble between 25 and 30 mph and then have the driver pick up the speed before they stand up. However, most barefooters tumble at a normal two-foot barefoot speed.

The tumbleturn should be one smooth, controlled movement. For a right turn, extend your arms and legs and begin swinging your legs to the front position by pulling the handle in an arc to the side toward your right thigh (toward your left thigh for a left turn). At the same time you initiate the pull, tuck your legs closer to your body. Keep your hip up by leading the turn with your feet and keeping your knees pointed away from the boat. This will keep your hip from catching the water which would stop the turn and/or roll you over. It is just like keeping the leading edge of a trick ski up when in a sideslide position.

The momentum of your turn should carry you until you are facing directly forward. At this point, you stand on your feet remembering to keep your knees bent and the handle in.

TIP

"The two most important things to remember are to lift your leading hip by turning your feet away from the boat, and to pull the handle

Begin on your stomach, riding on your forearms for stability.

Tuck your head and curl your shoulders up when on your back.

Pull the handle to your hip and turn your knees away from the boat.

Maintain your momentum until your feet are directly in front of you.

down to your hip or just below. Also, don't think about turning until the handle touches the hip. We find that it is best for a beginner to attempt the tumble at 25 mph. Once you get around forward, wait for the boat to accelerate to barefoot speed before standing up. The tumble is easier at a slow speed, and it reduces the amount of discomfort while the skier is riding on his back.

This trick requires a degree of strength, so you should only try a few of them at a time. There's no point in a beginner trying it unless they're fresh." **Mike Seipel**

Amen Mike! When I first learned it I could only make three or four tumbles each session before I would poop out!

Stand up, keeping your knees and arms bent.

Barefooting 51

START METHODS

Problem/Diagnosis

Problem: *Shoulders dig in when on back.*
Diagnosis: *Shoulders are down. Curl them up.*
Problem: *Get stuck sideways; cannot quite get around forward.*
Diagnosis: *1. You are not building enough momentum with your turn. 2. Leading hip might be catching water, concentrate on rolling leading hip up by turning knees away from the boat. 3. Pull legs around forcefully with the handle. 4. Finish turn by pulling handle to the center of your body.*

The Backward Step-Off Part One: Getting Backward On The Ski

Backward barefooting separates the men from the boys and is one of the biggest challenges an advancing barefooter will face. In all sincerity, do not even bother attempting a backward start unless you really want it. It does not come easy for most people, and the falls are often painfully memorable. The sight of a person traveling backward on his bare feet, leaning away at a 45-degree angle, and smothered in spray, makes this a feature act in many ski shows. In fact, the show skier must master the backward barefoot before he can qualify for "Ski One," the label that signifies the top position in this profession.

The first step to the backward barefoot is a trick in itself—learning to ski backward on a special back barefoot ski.

Types Of Skis

The widest variety of odd water skis isn't found at the Water Ski Hall of Fame in Winter Haven, Florida; it's found at any major barefoot tournament, particularly international ones. There you'll find backward barefoot (BBF) skis ranging from 40 inch trick skis to 72 inch jumpers. They can be made of honeycomb aluminum or plain old junk. I guess that's why they're often termed "freeboards"—not because they don't cost anything, but because they're not worth anything!

The long jump ski is the most stable ski. It is the easiest for the backward deepwater start and the ski walkaround, but it is the most difficult to turn around. On the other hand, a trick ski is the easiest to turn around, but is the least stable at 35 mph, the standard step-off speed. The stability of a trick ski can be increased by placing a fin at the front of the ski, so that when you turn around backward, the fin is in the water. The longer and narrower the trick ski, the more stability it has.

I never thought it could be done until I saw it: A guy turned around on a normal trick ski without a fin, accelerated to 40 mph, planted his foot and stepped off. That's like trying to balance on a bar of soap in the shower!

Setting Up The Ski

The typical American BBF ski is a normal wood "combo" ski with the bindings mounted backward and the heel piece removed. The bindings should be placed so that your feet are centered on the ski.

Make sure the tip of the ski is above the water.

Keep the handle behind your knees and knees bent.

52 Barefooting

The rear binding should place the rear foot as close to the front foot as possible. This makes a versatile ski which can be used for any of the three methods when preparing for a backward step-off. (It can also be used as a front step-off ski by placing your foot backward into the rear toe binding.)

Finally, no step-off ski would be complete without an array of stickers and graffiti. (Who cares how well it works as long as it looks good?)

Now let's talk about technique. Remember, your goal is to get backward on a ski that will be stable at 35 mph If you are a trick skier this may be easy. If you have never skied backward before, it may take some time. There are three common methods for getting backward on the ski: the backward deepwater start, the ski turnaround, and the ski walkaround. The backward deepwater start is the easiest.

The Backward Deepwater Start

Begin in a forward one-ski deepwater position with both feet in the ski, knees bent, and line tight. The driver should keep the line tight and drag you through the water as slowly as possible.

Now do a 180-degree turn and grab the handle behind your knees. The tip of the ski should be above the water as in a normal one-ski start. When you're as stable as you think you'll get (this position is always a little awkward), drop your head under the water as a signal for the drive to accelerate.

Keep the handle behind your knees, knees bent, and apply equal pressure to both feet. Too much pressure on your front foot will prevent the ski from planing properly, while too much pressure on your back foot might sink the nose of the ski.

A common problem that can throw you off balance is the skis pushing against the rope. This can be prevented by steering away from the rope slightly as you start. For example, if the rope is to the right of the ski, steer left.

Once you are skiing, stand up and bring the handle to the small of your back.

If you have trouble with this start, do it on two skis and then drop one. The technique is the same except that the rope is between the skis rather than to the side.

If you are going to use a boom, you can lower the boom near the water by placing several people on that side of the boat. You sit on the end of the boom with the ski underneath you. From this position, it's relatively easy to jump off the boom and to keep the ski tip above the surface of the water in front of the boom as you ski backward. From this position continue on as previously described.

The Ski Turnaround

The ski turnaround is the technique most commonly used in America. A trick ski with a fin makes this maneuver easy. If you use a longer ski, turning it 180 degrees will be more difficult but with practice, the turnaround can be performed easily and consistently.

Your weight and ski size will determine the speed you need for the turnaround. Generally this speed is 20-25 mph.

Begin by doing a forward deepwater start on the

Apply equal pressure to both feet.

Once skiing, stand up and bring the handle to the small of your back.

Barefooting 53

START METHODS

Begin with knees bent and lead the turn with your head.

Do a smooth and controlled turn.

Place front foot on top of binder (if binder is used).

Turn your back foot around and release one hand.

Keep the handle in close with back erect.

Finish with your eyes at the horizon, knees bent and handle near your body.

Slide your front foot around.

Grasp the handle with both hands.

START METHODS

Begin the turn with equal pressure on both feet. When you finish the turn, you should have slightly more weight on your front foot. As you turn, remember these trick skiing fundamentals: Begin and end with knees bent; look at the horizon; keep your back erect; finish with the handle held against the small of your back.

Some people merely slide the ski around without "unweighting" it at all. I prefer to unweight the ski by starting crouched and then rising up in my knees just before I begin the turn. Whichever method you use, do a smooth, controlled turn. Don't turn it too fast or "throw it."

The Ski Walkaround

As with the ski turnaround, the most comfortable speed for the ski walkaround is 20 to 25 mph. To execute the maneuver, first lift your back foot off the ski, turn it around and place it backward on the ski, being careful not to catch it in the spray. Letting go with one hand will make this easier, but be sure to keep the handle in close.

Shift your weight to the back foot and turn your front foot around backward by pivoting it on your toes. Your whole body should turn 180 degrees with this move so that you are now looking backward.

What's awkward about this preparation method? You end up with your feet reversed. If you started with your left foot as your front foot, it is now your back foot. Therefore most people will take what is now their front foot off the ski, and plant it in the water to prepare for the step-off. This keeps your most stable foot on the ski.

The Backward Step-Off Part Two: Stepping Off

As an enthusiastic self-taught recreational skier, it took me two years, over 300 attempts, and countless headaches before joining the elite group of backward barefooters. Unless you are a proficient trick skier, you too are likely to find the backward step-off to be one of the most challenging feats in all barefooting. However, the growing popularity of barefooting has resulted in a refinement of the ski. Since you have adapted the ski for this trick, it will go backward with the fin in the air. At this point, onlookers may question your intelligence.

teaching process so that now, with the use of a boom and proper instruction, a person with no trick skiing experience can be backward barefooting on a standard 75 foot line in just a week. (The second person ever to backward barefoot, Don Thompson, used this procedure with excellent results.)

Using the boom permits you to first hold directly onto it for maximum stability, then to go to a very short (five foot) line for moderate stability, and finally you get behind the boat on a normal-length line.

If you are not using a boom, you'll need to develop your balance on the ski before attempting to step off. Do this by skiing backward across the wakes and also by holding one foot in the air and steering back and forth inside the wake. The proper stance on the ski is knees bent, handle held tight against the small of your back, eyes on the horizon, and back erect. Most people tend to bend over too much at the waist.

One extra piece of equipment many backward barefooters are finding very helpful is a neck collar of the kind used in football. Backward falls at over 30 mph are literally a pain in the neck. The whiplash effect of slapping the water on your back time after time can result in pulled neck muscles. Many skiers have found that this whiplash effect can be reduced by using the neck collar.

If you choose to use a collar, it should be high in the back (some people even use two collars) and tied down snugly in the front.

So much for the preparation, let's take to the water.

When you are attempting the step-off behind the boat, the first question to be answered is, "Where do I step-off? Outside the left wake, outside the right wake or between the wakes?"

Wake characteristics will usually determine where you should be. Most tournament inboards and heavier ski boats have very turbulent wakes inside and nice troughs just outside the wake. Therefore, skiing in the trough at the end of a 75 foot line provides smooth water. It also allows you to brace against the wake with your bare foot for added stability. For example in planting your right foot, you should be to your left of the wake so that your foot will be "against" the wake. Vice versa for planting your left foot.

If your boat has smooth water inside the wake, you might find it easier for you there. The advantages inside the wake are that you get a straight pull rather than from an angle, and also the boat will smooth out any rough water.

Okay, you're in your selected spot. Begin with a boat speed of approximately 25 mph. The water is nice and soft at this speed making it easier to place the foot in the water.

Now plant your foot in the water about 12 inches to the side of the ski and 12 inches behind your foot on the ski. Although both knees should be bent slightly, the barefoot leg will be straighter than the ski leg.

The position of the ankle is important too. Your bare foot should be at an approximate 90-degree angle to your shin. Too little angle and your foot will be nearly level with the water, making it prone to catching a heel. Too much angle and your foot won't plane properly.

If you have difficulty getting a "plant," slow the boat speed a few miles per hour until the water is soft enough so that you can. If you have no problem getting a plant, it might be easier for you to plant at a higher speed so you can immediately place more weight on the foot. The faster you can comfortably plant, the better.

Once you are stable with your foot in the water, have the driver increase the speed. As the speed increases, transfer more and more weight onto your foot by rocking your hips and shoulders over your foot.

As you reach your step-off speed (backward one-foot speed or approximately three mph less than front one-foot speed, slower if on the boom) virtually all your weight should be on the bare foot with the body directly in line above it. Your shoulders, hips, and bare foot should be almost in a straight line, with not much bend at your waist. As you rock completely onto one-foot, the ski will drop away. Then gently place your foot on the water to obtain an approximately shoulder-width stance. This movement should be executed smoothly and slowly.

Once you establish the two-foot backward barefoot position, it is best to have the driver slow down three to five mph for more stability and less-painful falls.

Another style of back step-off, which some people prefer, is the "flick." The prestep-off position for the "flick" generally has a wider stance and a little more lean away from the boat than the "rock" technique previously described.

The actual step-off is a very clean small "flick" of the ski leg. With a slight movement you shift a little more of your weight onto your bare foot while straightening your ski leg and "flicking" or pushing the ski to the outside. The ski does not have to be picked up and kicked away. A slight shove is sufficient.

Once your leg is straightened, do not bend it and step back onto the water. Simply bring the foot back to the water, toes first, sliding it in from the side. You should end up in a stance slightly wider than your shoulder width.

The advantages to the "flick" method are that it can be executed at a much slower speed since your second foot quickly returns to the water providing instant support after leaving the ski. Full grown adults can execute this style step-off between 25-30 mph!

Also, because you never have a lot of weight on just one foot, this step-off is well suited for use in rough water. With the ski flicked well to the side, you are much less likely to get tangled with the ski, too.

TIP

"Learning on a boom is best, but if no boom is available you must become very stable backward on a ski behind the boat. A few falls on the ski also prepares you for 35 mph backward barefoot falls.

"Relaxing your arms and letting the handle out slightly allows the pull to come from your shoulders and keeps you from tiring too quickly.

"Don't go fast enough to actually be able to one foot. That's bad because you get into the habit of only having stability on one leg. The slower speed forces you to place weight on the second foot.

"The second foot (the foot coming off the ski) must be placed in the water up equal to the other foot. Finally the weight is equalized on both feet."   **Ron Scarpa**

START METHODS

In the top row, the skier uses a narrow stance with all his weight placed on one foot. In the bottom row, the skier uses a wider stance and places slightly more than half of his weight on the bare foot and "flicks" the ski to one side.

Barefooting 59

START METHODS

TIP

"Start directly on the boom first. When you can make it three times on the boom, go to a five foot extension. When you can make it three times on the extension, go behind the boat.

"When trying it on the boom, the boat should be balanced so that the boom is four inches above your hips (slightly above the waist). Ski quite a while on the boom to become very comfortable before attempting to step-off. The boat speed for planting your foot on the boom is only 20-25 mph. Step-off speed should be no faster than 30 mph.

"There are two things to do at this point. One, push the foot in the water as far out in front of you as you can (ahead of the boom), and two, crouch down very low. This is a strong plant position.

"As the speed is increased to about 30 mph, all you have to do is lean over on to the bare foot and the ski will slide off your foot. It is actually easier to ski away on one foot than on two feet. Then very, very slowly put the other foot in the water. As soon as you learn this, learn to ski equally on both feet or you'll develop a bad habit of skiing unsymmetrically.

"It is very important to look out at the horizon. This provides a reference point to tell you if you're tilted one way or another.

"The only difference when going from the boom to the extension to the long rope is balance.

"When planting, most people need to keep their foot as flat as possible on the water by pulling the toes up hard toward their shins. The water should also be hitting you right in the middle of your foot." **Mike Seipel**

Problem/Diagnosis

Problem: *Catching a heel when planting.*
Diagnosis: *1. Applying too much weight before sufficient speed is attained. 2. Foot is not far enough ahead of you. 3. Foot is too level with the water, making the heel low. Flex your ankle or bend your knee to raise your heel.*
Problem: *Fall on your face.*
Diagnosis: *1. You are looking down. Keep your eyes on the horizon. 2. Bending at the waist too much. 3. Leaning away too far from the boat.*

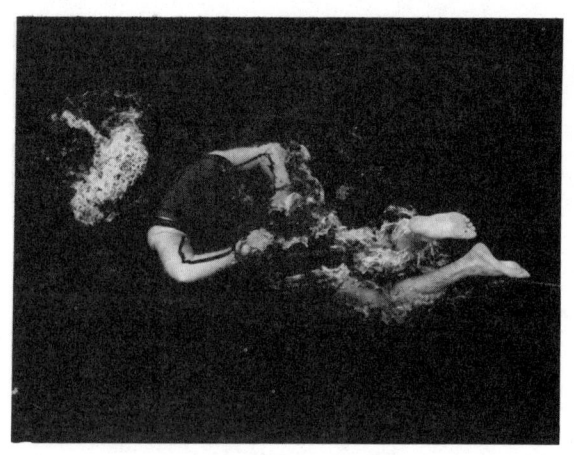

Begin with one foot on the rope and arch your back as the boat begins to pull.

4. Too much speed.
Problem: *Catching a heel when stepping off.*
Diagnosis: *1. Too erect. Lean away a little more. 2. Transferring too much weight to one foot. 3. Not placing second foot out equal to the first foot.*

Backward Deepwater Start

In 1974 it was my turn. No instruction, no clues, no intuition—just determination guided me. In those days, the only barefoot instruction came from the School of Hard Knocks. After six months of trial and error, I finally experienced the thrill of victory over the backward deepwater or "back deep" start.

The best procedure for learning this maneuver is to use a five foot rope on the boom. The boom eliminates your having to contend with the stern rollers. Stern rollers are waves that are created when the boat planes off and move perpendicular to the boat's path. Stern rollers are the nemesis of barefooters doing "back deeps".

In addition to foiling these rollers, the boom provides lift when you're attempting to stand up. However, if you don't have a boom, that's okay. A "back deep" can be learned successfully behind the boat, too.

I also recommend a regular 11-inch handle for skiers learning this maneuver. When you release it, the shorter handle will be less likely to hit your calves or heels than a 14 or 15 inch handle.

A barefoot wetsuit is almost essential for "back deeps," although a normal full-length wetsuit or a

60 Barefooting

Take your foot off the rope as the water lifts your legs.

Curl your elbows and shoulders down and stiffen your legs as you plane.

Spread your legs wide and turn your toes out to prepare to plant.

Ease both feet into the water and bend at the waist to stand up.

"shorty" wetsuit with leg straps can be used.

The only other piece of equipment required for guys—and I mean *required*—is a hockey cup (or "cricket box," depending on what side of the Atlantic you're on). It won't take many tries without one for you to realize its importance.

There are three primary steps to the back deepwater: (1) the preparatory position in the water, (2) planing and acceleration, (3) planting your feet and standing up.

STEP 1 Begin in a forward deepwater position on your back with the boat moving forward just fast enough to keep the line tight. Then roll onto your stomach, grasp the handle behind your back, and immediately hook one foot over the rope. The hooked foot will keep the rope from pulling you over backward. Keep the handle pinned to the small of your back throughout the start.

When you are stable, signal the driver to go by yelling "hit it" and then ducking your head underwater. The driver should hesitate a second for you to get set and then begin a very gradual acceleration.

NOTE: I recommend a verbal "hit it" followed by ducking the head for a good reason: The common alternatives are potentially dangerous. For example, yelling "go" can be misinterpreted as "no" or "whoa." And using just a head duck as a signal is bad because sometimes the skier will unintentionally duck his head when he's not ready.

Barefooting **61**

START METHODS

STEP 2 The instant you feel the first pull of the boat, arch your body and take your foot off the line. Being in this arched position will cause the water to lift your legs up so that you won't be pulled over backward and keep your head up so that you won't get a snout full of water.

As you begin to plane, stiffen your legs by pointing your toes toward the boat as hard as you can. Curl your elbows and shoulders down. This will cause you to ride on your abdominal area, and your shoulders will act as a trim tab to keep you from bouncing. Remain very stiff, keeping your legs lifted up as high as you can while trying to place weight on your shoulders.

Practice riding on your stomach for a while before you try planting your feet. You should be able to ride at about 20 to 25 mph.

NOTE: If you experience a lot of drag before planing off, bend down at the waist slightly but resume the arched position as soon as you plane.

STEP 3 When you're able to ride comfortably to within five mph of your minimum backward speed (the minimum backward speed is 25 to 30 mph for most adults), spread your legs very wide, pull your toes back toward your shins as far as possible and externally rotate your feet about 45 degrees. Ease both feet into the water simultaneously. In the proper position, the feet will not jab into the water; instead, they will go in smoothly. Once you establish a plant, the driver should accelerate up to your minimum backward speed.

To stand up, bend at the waist and push down with your chest. Thinking about bringing your feet toward your shoulders may help to do this. Once you are clearly on your feet, the driver can accelerate to your normal barefoot speed. Finally, bring your feet together and torso up to a normal stance.

You can develop the feel of the stand-up by reversing the sequence of the start. While skiing in the backward barefoot position (from another start method), have the boat slow to your minimum barefoot speed. Lean away from the boat, spread your legs and turn your feet out. Lower your chest to the water by bending at the waist. Go all the way down until you touch your chest to the water and pick your feet up so that you will be totally planing on your stomach.

TIP

"I recommend planting your feet right away (10 mph) rather than planting at a higher speed. This eliminates the common problem of porpoising experienced in the 10-15 mph range. It also reduces the wear and tear from learning to ride up to 25 mph on your stomach.

In order to plane correctly, straighten your legs hard with your toes turned toward the outside and your feet close together. Jam your hips hard into the water. Accelerate to only 10 mph.

"When planting your feet, there are two important things to do: Pull your toes back hard toward your shin, and spread your legs wide. It is very important that you do not to make any effort to plant your feet in the water. All you have to do is push your chest and chin into the water. By doing this, your feet will be in the perfect position to go into the water smoothly. Ride this position for awhile to get a feel for it.

"When you are comfortable and relaxed, slowly begin to accelerate. With slight pressure on your chin and chest, the leverage will automatically pull you up.

"When going to the long line from the boom, the maneuver is performed exactly the same except it takes much longer to stand up after you plant because you don't have the lift from the boom." **Mike Seipel**

"The proper position to ride on your stomach is with the handle held high on your back, legs lifted high off the water (arched from the waist to the feet), and toes pulled back (as if in toe-hold straps). Your toes should be turned out with your heels together.

"Plant your feet between 20-25 mph. After you plant, let your arms out and drop the handle down over your butt. This allows your butt to come up between your arms and also helps keep you tracking straight.

"Don't look down, keep your eyes open and look at the horizon." **Ron Scarpa**

Problem/Diagnosis

Problem: *You get pulled over backward before planing off.*
Diagnosis: *1. Foot is not on the rope. 2. Not arching enough. 3. Arms are extended.*
Problem: *You bounce or "porpoise".*
Diagnosis: *1. Shoulders and elbows are not down enough. 2. Body is loose: be stiff as a board. 3. Maybe try planting your feet right away.*
Problem: *Knees and legs dig into the water when planing on stomach.*
Diagnosis: *1. Back is not arched enough to lift thighs and legs. Lean away from boat more onto your chest. 2. Going too fast. 3. Legs spread too soon.*
Problem: *Feet jerk and skip out when trying to plant them into the water.*
Diagnosis: *1. Legs not spread enough. Many people who are not very flexible have to spread them as wide as possible. 2. Feet are not turned out. 3. Feet not pulled back toward shins.*
Problem: *Feet are planted but cannot stand up.*
Diagnosis: *1. Not enough speed, or too much speed. 2. Feet not planted deep enough in water. Put more weight on them by bending at the waist. 3. Feet spread too wide. 4. Not pushing with your chest and bending at the waist.*

Backward Beach Start

If you have mastered the backward deepwater start, the backward beach start will be a piece of cake. You do not need as much speed off the beach as a forward beach start, so lying down about 10 feet from the water's edge should be adequate.

The backward beach starting position.

Take several forward steps.

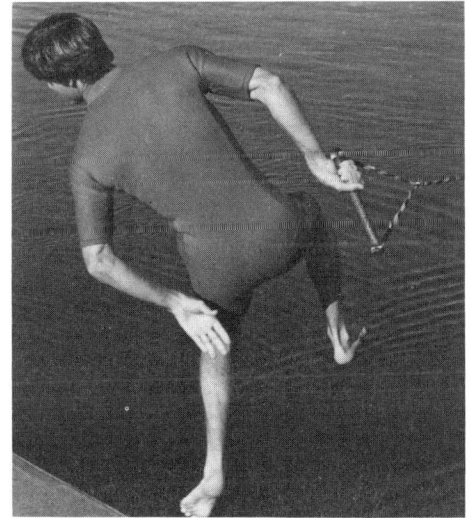

Push off and turn to the backwards horizontal position.

Land arched and continue as you would for the backward deepwater start.

Barefooting 63

START METHODS

Lie down on your stomach in the planing position outlined in the backward deepwater start: Handle in small of your back, shoulders and elbows down, back arched, head up. The only difference is that you hook one foot over the rope with your feet spread about 12 inches apart. This will keep you from getting pulled over backward when being dragged down the beach.

Have the driver pull you gently off the beach and into the water. Once you are planing, take your foot off the rope and continue as in steps four and five of a backward deepwater start.

Backward Flying Dock Start

To receive credit for a flying dock start in competition, you are only required "to make a distinct movement toward an airborne position." Technically, this can be done by merely falling off the side of a dock into a backward deepwater position and finishing with a regular backward deepwater start. It is legal and might be the most consistent technique for competition. However, a true flying backward dock start is not only fun, but spectators love it.

Begin with a tight line, four or five steps from the edge of the dock. Have the driver fast idle, pulling you down the dock about five to eight mph. When you reach the edge, push off, turn your body around backward and land on your stomach. When performing this: (1) Pull the handle to the small of your back, (2) do not under-turn or over-turn, you need to land squarely, and (3) land with your back arched as in step two of the backward deepwater start.

After you land in the water, have the driver begin accelerating as in a backward deepwater. To complete the maneuver, follow steps three, four and five of a backward deepwater start.

Backward Tumbleturn Start

Changes in tournament rules have made this start nearly obsolete. But because this is a complete book on barefooting, I had to include it, even though I dislike the start. (Maybe because I fell on it in two World Tournaments!)

The handle used for a backward tumbleturn is modified with the addition of a small handle or "peg" about four feet from the handle which the

Use your elbow on the water for stability.

skier can grab for stability. With the main handle below your rear, hold the peg so that your arm has a slight bend in it.

Make your turn to the direction that feels best to you. For a turn to the left, grab the peg with your right hand. With the bridle passing underneath your right arm and over your back, grip the handle behind you with your left hand. Your left hand with the handle should be held below your left buttock.

Roll over to your back and signal the driver to gently pull you out of the water. Take the pull equally with both hands. After you begin to be pulled, roll to your stomach and use your elbow and knees on the water for stability. Digging one elbow in the water will keep you from bouncing.

The speed you choose to tumble is strictly a personal preference, but you should be planing comfortably on the surface so that you can spin easily. This is usually between 20-25 mph. When you are ready to turn:

1. Take all the pull of the rope in your left hand.
2. Initiate the turn by pushing the rope to the right.
3. Simultaneously arch your back and lean onto your chest, picking your thighs and legs up off the water.
4. Lift up on your right side so that it will not catch the water.
5. Slide your hand down the rope to control your spin and guide your hand to the handle.

As you reach the backward position, pull the handle to the small of your back. Do not worry about properly gripping the handle. Most people

64 Barefooting

Arch your body and lean away as you begin the turn.

Slide your hand down the rope.

Grasp the handle to stop rotating.

Continue as you would for a backward deepwater start.

will go ahead and stand up with their right hand either holding the rope or upside down on the handle. Continue as in a backward deepwater.

Problem/Diagnosis

Problem: *Bouncing when on stomach.*
Diagnosis: *1. Push knees and elbow into the water.*
Problem: *You dig into the water and roll over when sideways.*
Diagnosis: *1. Not turning with your right side lifted up. 2. Not arching and picking your thighs and legs off the water. 3. Not enough boat speed.*

Problem: *Overturning 180 degrees.*
Diagnosis: *1. Too fast of a spin. Turn slower. 2. Not stopping the turn with your right hand on the handle.*
Problem: *Underturning 180 degrees.*
Diagnosis: *1. Turning too slowly. 2. Not arched enough which allows legs to catch water, stopping your rotation.*
Problem: *Digging into the water and getting pulled over when backward.*
Diagnosis: *1. Arms outstretched when reaching backward position. 2. Not arched and leaning away on chest. 3. Not a smooth transition to attaining the backward position.*

Barefooting **65**

START METHODS

Backward One-Foot Stand-Up Start

The backward one-foot stand-up is undoubtedly one of the toughest start methods. Once you master this start, you will have moved into the highest ranks of barefooters. Much of the struggle is maintaining control while planing on your stomach at speeds in excess of 35 mph. Here are a few helpful tips:

1. Be sure to arch your body, lifting thighs up off the water.

2. Keep feet close together.

3. If you begin to get pulled over, take the foot you will be planting in the water and place it on the rope. To receive credit for the start in competition, the foot in the air must not touch the water or the rope.

The speed for planting should be two to four mph slower than your normal backward one-foot speed. Although some people wait until full one-foot speed before planting, you'll find that it's easier to plant your foot at a slower speed and you'll have more control on your stomach. The only drawback is that you have to rely on the boat driver to give you a few additional mph after planting your foot.

Start this maneuver like the normal backward deepwater start. Get a good grip on the rope and lock it in the small of your back. When you are ready to plant, pull the front of your foot all the way back toward your shin. Keep your feet close together and plant your foot gently in the water straight up and down, directly underneath the rope. The leverage of your leg will naturally pull you up, but stay low, waiting for more speed. Keep your shoulders level and avoid bending at the waist too much.

TIP

"To ride on your stomach at a higher speed, arch your legs up hard and lean away. If you don't, you will tend to be pulled over backward.

"When ready to plant, center the handle over the leg you will be standing on, and let the handle out over your butt. It is important that you place your foot in the water very gently. Also, as you stand up, keep the lifted leg centered near the rope, not out to the side."

Ron Scarpa

Arch hard, leaning away from the boat, and keep your feet close together.

Plant your foot directly underneath the rope.

66 Barefooting

Problem/Diagnosis

Problem: *Keep getting pulled over backward when on your stomach.*
Diagnosis: *1. Legs too far apart. 2. Not arched and leaning away from the boat.*
Problem: *You are pulled to one side or the other when planting.*
Diagnosis: *1. Foot is not directly underneath the rope. 2. Foot is not straight up and down.*
Problem: *You fall to one side when standing up.*
Diagnosis: *1. Foot is not planted directly underneath the rope. 2. Shoulders are not kept level. 3. Legs and knees too far apart.*

The leverage of your leg will naturally pull you up.

Keep your shoulders level and avoid bending at the waist too much.

START METHODS

Backward Toe-Hold Stand-Up

The backward toe-hold stand-up is not as difficult as a regular backward one-foot stand-up, but it looks more impressive to unknowledgeable spectators. It is easier mainly because your arms are free and you can actually push on the water with your hands to correct your balance. However, you *do not* push yourself up with your hands as it may appear.

A good quality, comfortable toe-strap is important. Avoid the "bear trap" style strap that closes on your feet, and use a loosely fitting strap instead. If you find it difficult to keep the strap from sliding off your foot, gradually tighten it until it just barely stays on—no tighter. When learning, it is better to have the strap slip off a few times than risk injury. A safety release should be used in the boat as a back up.

In deep water with the line tight, place the strap all the way up your foot. Roll over onto your stomach and put your head underwater to signal the driver to go. As the boat begins to pull, put your free foot up into the air by bending at the knee, and then lift up your toe-strap foot. (If both feet are underwater, you will not plane off.)

There is no particular body position for planing off, just let the boat pull you out. Concentrate on keeping the strap on by bringing your toes back toward your shin. Once you are planing, use your hands on the water to keep from bouncing.

The speed to plant your foot is a matter of personal preference. However, I recommend that you try to plant five to eight mph below your normal backward one-foot speed. (At a slightly slower speed, you will have more control and find it easier to plant.) Plant your foot straight up and down directly beneath the rope. In order to do this, it will feel like you almost have to cross your legs.

Planting your foot will signal the driver to increase to your normal one-foot speed. Stay low, using your hands for balance while waiting for more speed. Begin to rise up when you feel the water is firm enough to support your weight. Bending the knee of the leg you are standing on will help your balance.

Hold your free foot in the air for take off.

Problem/Diagnosis

Problem: *You roll over or move outside the wake after planting.*
Diagnosis: *1. Foot is not directly underneath rope. 2. Foot is not directly straight up and down. 3. Shoulders are not level.*
Problem: *You fall over to the side while standing.*
Diagnosis: *1. Foot is not directly beneath you. 2. Bend your water leg for better stability.*

Use your hands for control while planing.

Plant your foot directly underneath the rope.

Stay low waiting for increased speed.

Bend your knee while rising up.

START METHODS

The Front Toe Stand-Up

The beauty of this start is that, although it is one of the two most difficult starts and virtually every top skier needs to know it to be competitive, it can still be accomplished by a non-backward barefooter. If you are solid in the forward toe-hold position, you are capable of making this start.

The method for learning is to reverse the procedure. First attain the forward toe-hold position at a slow forward toe-hold speed. Grab your strap leg (the one holding the rope) behind the knee, with your hand on that same side. This will help to keep your upper body forward without having to rely solely on your abdominal muscles.

Now begin crouching low to the water while staying forward over the skiing foot. Reach down to the water with your free hand, palm forward and fingers trailing (supine position). Sit as low as possible without having to transfer weight from your foot to your butt. Finally, go ahead and sit onto the water lifting your foot off the water. This reverse procedure will help you to obtain a feel for the positions you will be experiencing.

Now you are skimming across the water on your gluteus maximus at your minimum toe-hold or one-foot speed (my massive 140 pounds requires 38 to 39 mph). You are leaning back slightly and gripping your strap leg just behind a slightly bent knee. Your free hand is on the surface of the water behind you and to the side. Your free foot is just above the surface of the water, just forward of your knee.

The action begins and three things happen simultaneously: (1) Rock as far forward as possible (or, as Mike Seipel says, "Rock forward until you think you're going to go out the front, then go a little further."), (2) Push your foot deep into the water, "as though you wanted to push it straight to the bottom," Mike says. Push it straight down, not out in front. (3) Use a forward sweeping action on the water with your free hand. This will help to push you up and forward, and it will also cause your free hand side shoulder to drop, a necessary ingredient for this trick. Dropping the shoulder allows you to center your weight over the skiing foot.

You're up! The technique is the same behind the boat, but it is more difficult to get forward over the foot.

Grip the strap leg behind your knee.

Rock as far forward as possible.

Push your foot deep ing the water with you

70 Barefooting

Problem/Diagnosis

Problem: *Not able to get all the way up onto the foot.*
Diagnosis: *1. Not rocking forward hard enough and/or far enough. 2. Not pushing foot into the water hard enough. 3. Foot is planted too far out in front of you.*
Problem: *Keep falling over toward your strap-leg side.* **Diagnosis:** *1. Not dropping your shoulder and leaning over the bare foot enough. 2. Bare foot is not under the rope.*

to the water, sweep-free hand.

Stay forward over your skiing foot.

You're up!

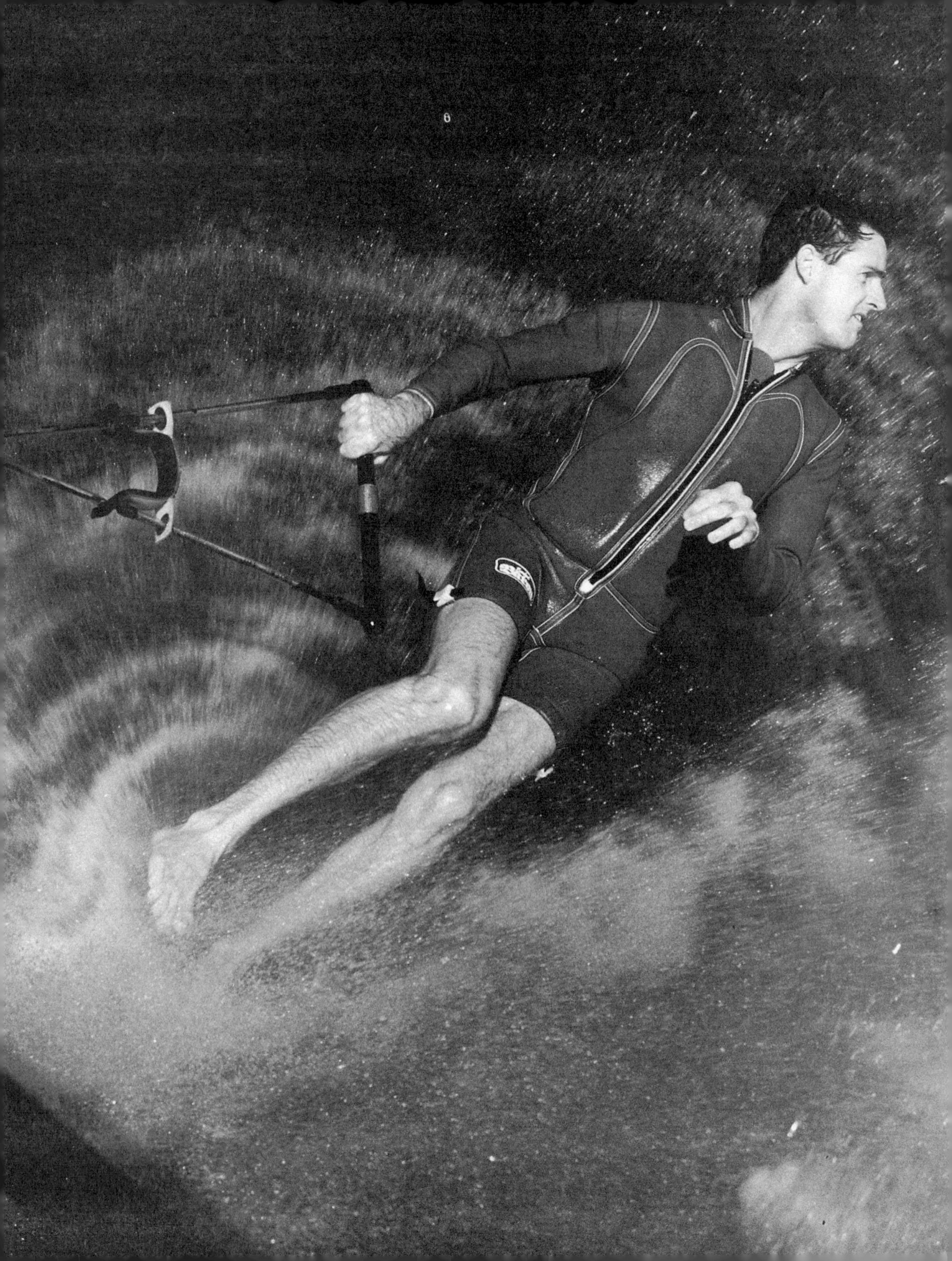

TRICKS

Tricks are the most challenging competitive skiing event, requiring balance, coordination, and many hours of hard practice. A trick champion is due the utmost respect for his ability. With many new tricks being developed each year in this very progressive event, it is no wonder that barefooters are doing tricks on their feet that many people are still trying to master on skis!

Barefoot tricks need not be regarded only as a competitive event. Even if you never plan to enter a tournament, tricks are fun to do. In smoother water, there are few barefooters that would not try to pick up one foot, or try one of numerous tricks that are now being performed.

In competition the contestant is allotted two 15-second time periods or "passes" in which to attempt as many different tricks as he or she desires. Each trick has a predetermined point value based on its difficulty. A fall concludes the individual pass, with points being scored for tricks done correctly before the fall. The points from both passes are totaled, and the contestant with the most points wins. Today, barefooters are completing as many as 25 tricks in 30 seconds, racking up scores in excess of 4000 points.

One-Foot

One-footing is the most basic of all tricks and it is easy if the proper technique is used. With improper technique even an experienced skier will have trouble with it. Calm water is especially important when learning to one-foot, so position yourself outside the wake. It is easiest to pick up the foot closest to the wake. Even if the speed is sufficient it will feel as though your foot is sinking a bit. Do not let that "psyche you out," go ahead and boldly pick up the foot.

Proper one foot form with shoulders back and legs bent.

The author performing a one foot front-to-back.

A common example of poor positioning: legs straight, body bent forward at the waist and skiing foot pushed out too far in front.

Barefooting 73

TRICKS

1. Speed: five mph above your normal barefoot speed.
2. Assume a fairly erect position with your arms slightly bent, shoulders back from your hips, and your feet very close together (almost touching).
3. Shift all your weight onto one foot.
4. The skiing foot should be directly underneath the rope.
5. Pick your foot straight up off the water, keeping it close to your shin.
6. You may need to "edge" or steer away from the wake slightly to keep from getting pulled into it. Do this by turning your shoulders, hips, and foot away from the wake.

Problem/Diagnosis

Problem: *Lots of spray and very unstable.*
Diagnosis: *1. Leaning back too far when picking up your foot. This is frequently caused by lifting the foot with with your knee straight rather than keeping the foot close to your supporting leg 2. Skiing leg too straight. Bend the knee.*
Problem: *Constantly falling down onto the lifted foot.*
Diagnosis: *1. Picking foot up to the side. Keep it close to the supporting leg. 2. Not centering your weight over the foot in the water. 3. Skiing foot is not under the rope.*

Toe-hold

Toe-hold barefooting is fun. Standing up high and clear while skimming across glass-calm water with your upper body relaxed and arms free is one of the most exhilarating sensations in all of barefooting. If you have good control barefooting on one foot, toe-hold barefooting is easy for you to learn.

You will need a special barefoot toe-hold handle for this trick. There are several manufacturers of these handles and they may be found at local water ski accessories shops. The barefoot toe-hold handle differs from a regular water ski toe-handle in that there is more length between the handle and toe-strap on a barefoot handle. This allows the barefooter to place his foot in the strap while keeping his shoulders back and strap leg fairly straight. Although it is possible to use a regular water ski toe-hold assembly, you have to go into the trick in a very awkward bent-over position. Also, most water ski toe straps are "bear traps," meaning they close tightly on the foot. This is unnecessary as well as dangerous for barefooting.

One more feature of the barefoot toe handle is plastic tubing placed over the rope between the handle and the toe-strap. This keeps the assembly rigid, preventing the handle from falling out of reach after it is released.

Optimally, when you are in the toe-hold position, the length of the toe-hold assembly will place the handle at about your knee. Most manufacturers make only one length of toe-hold handle, so if you have extra long or short legs you may have difficulty with the handle. If this is the case, or if your budget doesn't allow $50 or so to invest in a barefoot bridle, with a little rope splicing know-how it is easy to make a homemade model that will do the job fine.

Two additional things you will need to make the learning process easier is very calm water and a fast one-foot boat speed. These two conditions will allow you to stand up nice and high on your foot without worrying about catching a toe and the subsequent eyelid-peeling face plant.

Because of the need for calm water it is preferable to learn the toe-hold barefoot outside the wake. (I do not recommend using a boom because

Keep the skiing leg bent and underneath you.

the short line can cause instability.) It also makes a significant difference which side of the wake you try it on. If you are a strong left-foot one-footer you should try it on the left side of the wake, and vice-versa for the right foot. When outside the wake the rope does not pull you straight, but pulls at an angle toward the wake. When a left-footer is on the left of the wake and is pulled by his right leg, the pull of the rope opens his hips slightly, allowing him to easily keep his body and bare foot steering straight ahead. If he is on the right of the wake the pull of the rope will turn his right leg toward the wake and close his hips. The closed hips will tend to turn his hips, body, and bare foot to the left, causing him to drift into the wake.

Just as experienced barefooters overcome this problem of being pulled into the wake, so can beginners. But the fewer problems you have to deal with in the beginning, the better.

Okay, you're skimming across the glass-calm water at a hot one-foot speed. Begin with your feet close together, knees slightly bent, torso straight up and down, arms bent, handle at waist level, gripping the handle with both palms facing down. This general position should be maintained throughout the trick. The only significant change is raising the foot to the strap.

The first step is to begin one-footing. As you raise the foot to the strap there is a tendency to lean back. The key is to keep your body weight forward over the bare foot, because when you are pulled by your leg the low pull will cause you to lean back even farther. So keep your weight forward as you place the foot in the strap, but not by bending forward at the waist.

I see so many people trying to lean forward like this and it is all wrong! Although it may get your weight forward, it also causes you to push your bare foot out in front of you. You need to keep your hips over foot as well. In fact, your shoulders, hips, and bare foot should almost be in a straight line. Keep your back erect.

The foot should be placed as far in the strap as possible, not just on the toes. There is a great deal of pull, and the strap will come off easily if it is not high on the foot.

Once you attain this position, releasing the handle is easy. The key to this is to do it slowly and learned first.

1. Speed: three to four mph faster than your normal barefoot speed.

2. Crouch low.

Release the handle slowly and stay forward over your foot.

A common problem is being bent over at the waist with the skiing foot pushed out in front too far.

TRICKS

again staying forward keeping the hips tucked in underneath you. Keep your hands close to the handle in the beginning to avoid making any changes in body position. Once you are stable, go ahead and raise your hands clearly from the handle, wave to mom, smile, and enjoy the ride.

Problem/Diagnosis

Problem: *Constantly falling backwards.*
Diagnosis: *1. Weight is too far back. Bring your shoulders forward and foot underneath you.*
2. Throwing your arms and shoulders back after releasing the handle. Make only small and smooth body movements.
Problem: *Strap constantly slips off.*
Diagnosis: *Place your foot all the way into the strap and curl your toes and foot back toward your shin. Release the pressure slowly.*
(Note: Also refer back to One-Foot "Problem/Diagnosis").

Surface Jump And Wake Jump

The surface jump simply involves jumping up from the surface of the water, while the wake jump uses the wake to help lift you. The surface jump is

Steer gently toward the wake.

Crouch low.

Spring up, keeping your arms bent.

76 Barefooting

Time your spring at the top of the crest.

Stay over your feet, absorbing the landing with your knees.

Lift your feet up by bending your knees.

Absorb the landing in your knees, keeping arms bent and handle at waist level.

TRICKS

3. Give a quick spring and then pick your feet up in the air by bending your knees.
4. Land with arms bent, handle low, and absorb the landing in your knees.

This trick is easy if you spring up and not back. Landing softly by using the knees as shock absorbers is important.

Problem/Diagnosis

Problem: *Not leaving the water.*
Diagnosis: *Not springing hard enough and/or not picking your feet up off the water. Go for it!*
Problem: *Catching toes on landing.*
Diagnosis: *Landing too far forward or too stiff, i.e., not absorbing the landing in the knees.*

Landings may not always be on your feet, but you can still ride away from a "rear landing." The wake jump is performed the same way except you will be crossing over the wake and using it to give you more height.

1. Cross from outside the wake to inside when learning.
2. Drift gently toward the wake. Do not cut at it.
3. Spring up by extending your legs as you reach the top of the wake.

If you are not achieving extra height, you may be springing before or after the top of the wake. Concentrate on your timing and develop a "feel" for the wake. Problem/Diagnosis for wake jump same as surface jump.

Sit on the water and let your legs swing to the side.

Tumbleturns

The tumbleturn is probably the most versatile barefoot trick you can learn. It can be executed as a start method by planing off on your stomach, rolling over onto your back and then swinging your legs around forward to stand up. Once you are up on your feet, the tumbleturn can be done as a trick. In fact, barefoot trick competition recognizes four tumbleturn variations: two kinds of 180s and two kinds of 360s. The 180-degree tumbleturn consists of rolling over onto your back, stopping, and then rolling in the opposite direction as you return to the forward position. A reverse 180-degree tumbleturn is accomplished by doing all of the same movements but in the opposite direction of the first tumble.

The 360-degree tumbleturn is a non-stop movement. You roll over onto your back and continue your momentum around to the front position. A reverse 360-degree tumble can also be done. Tumbleturns can also be used to recover from a fall, **but only if it is a slow, controlled fall. Holding on to a hard straight forward fall can be dangerous.**

This can really surprise some unsuspecting drivers and observers. They see you fall and begin slowing down to turn the boat around and pick you up—and suddenly they see you back on your feet! The quick 360-degree tumbleturn is also an easy yet flamboyant trick that spectators love.

Keep your shoulders and head curled up, body tucked and handle in close.

You should learn the tumbleturn start before attempting it as a trick (see page 50) A barefoot wetsuit will make these tricks easier and less painful on the back.

The first step is lying down on the water from a barefoot position. This may take some courage at first, but it is actually very easy.

1. Speed: normal two-foot barefoot speed or slower.

2. Sit on the water by bending the knees past 90 degrees. Keep your arms bent.

3. Let your feet swing around to the side, and bring the handle over your head.

4. Keep your shoulders from digging in by curling your shoulders up.

When you are comfortable doing this, you will want to blend all the moves into one, so the sitting and rolling to your back becomes one fluid movement.

Once you are on your back the next steps are the same as the tumbleturn start. You should have learned that already, so I will not explain it here. If you haven't, go back and learn it.

TIP

"For a smooth transition from your feet to your back you must 1. really bend your knees and sit as low as possible, and 2. lean back and let your feet go to one side or the other."

Mike Seipel

360-Degree Tumble Turn

The 360-degree tumble consists of joining the rolling to your back and the tumbling up movements into one continuous movement. In a way it is actually easier than a single 180-degree tumble, because you are continuing the momentum of your swing through a complete 360-degrees while in the 180-degree tumble you have to stop and re-initiate the swing.

1. Speed: Normal barefoot speed.

2. Roll to your back.

3. As you approach the back position, keep in the tucked position and shift the handle slightly to the other side, still keeping it close to your middle.

4. Continue on around to the forward position and replant your feet.

KEY: Keep the handle near your waist throughout the trick.

As emphasized in the tumble-turn start, there are many people who do tumble turns, but very few who do them properly. Most people beat themselves silly trying to muscle their way through. The key to tumble turns is to lift the leading hip off the water enabling you to easily slide around forward. Turning your knees away from the boat will help facilitate this. If the leading hip digs in, it will act as a brake, slowing your spin.

Keep your momentum while swinging to the front position.

Plant your feet and stand up!

TRICKS

Problem/Diagnosis

Problem: *Not able to continue momentum past position on back.*
Diagnosis: *Not remaining in tuck position. Keep balled up with handle held in close throughout the turn.*
Problem: *Momentum stops at approximately the 270-degree position.*
Diagnosis: *Leading hip is down and catching the water and/or legs are extended. Keep the leading hip up and legs tucked in close to your body.*

(Problem/Diagnosis for the 180 tumbleturn is the same as the tumbleturn start, Page 51.)

Rope-On-Neck And Rope-In-Teeth

I DISCOURAGE DOING NECK AND TEETH TRICKS, AND SO DO MOST DENTISTS AND ORTHOPEDIC PHYSICIANS! Common sense tells you the potential is there for serious injury. I only include them in the book so that people who are going to do them will do them properly.

Proper equipment is a necessity. Use a forward toehold handle assembly with a 14-inch long handle and rigid plastic tubing over the rope. There must be plenty of room between the toestrap and handle. The teeth strap should be made of material free of anything that might snag a tooth, and should be long enough to reach the molars (rear teeth). A safety release is mandatory, operated by an observer familiar with the tricks. However, barefoot falls are so fast that even using a release may not prevent injury. Here are some tips fundamental to rope-on-neck and rope-in-teeth:

1. Speed should be your normal one-foot speed.
2. Attain barefoot position before placing rope on neck or rope in teeth.
3. Grip the plastic tubing on the sides of the handle.
4. Assume a position with shoulders well back from hips.

80 Barefooting

5. Knees bent so that feet are planing smoothly rather than pushing through the water.
6. Release the handle slowly.
7. Keep your hands near the handle.

For Rope-In-Teeth:
1. Bite teeth strap mostly with your molars.
2. Allow your head to tilt forward with the pull, but keep your shoulders back.

For Rope-On-Neck:
1. Place handle on neck, not on head (Takes total commitment).
2. Keep your head tilted back slightly.

Problem/Diagnosis

Problem: *Not enough strength to pull the handle to mouth or or behind neck.*
Diagnosis: *You are gripping the tubing too close to the handle. Grip it closer to the toe strap.*
Problem: *Cannot stay leaning away-pulled over forwards.*
Diagnosis: *1. Legs are straight, causing your feet to plow through the water rather than skim over the surface. Bend your knees to level your feet.*
2. Keep your shoulders well back from your hips.

For neck or Teeth One-foot:
1. Maintain the same two-foot stance, except with feet close together, and grip the tubing for balance and safety.
2. Pick up foot, bringing it close to your opposite knee.
3. For better balance and control, turn your hips toward the foot you are picking up, but keep the foot close to your opposite knee.
4. Slowly release your hands from the tubing.

Problem/Diagnosis

Problem: *Constantly falling down onto the foot you are attempting to lift.*
Diagnosis: *Weight not centered over foot in water. Keep lifted foot above supporting leg.*

Barefooting 81

TRICKS

Backward One-Foot

If you are a stable backward barefooter, backward one-foot will be as easy as forward one-foot.

1. Speed: Approximately 2 mph less than forward one-foot speed.
2. Assume a fairly erect backward barefoot stance.
3. Keep eyes looking up at horizon.
4. Hold handle against your back or buttock.
5. Bring feet together, almost touching.
6. Shift your weight to one foot.
7. Slowly pick up foot, keeping knees close together.

Key: Keep an erect stance with shoulders, hips, and feet almost in a straight line. Don't bend at the waist excessively.

Problem/Diagnosis

Problem: *Leaning away excessively and falling onto your face.*
Diagnosis: *1. You are looking down at the water. Keep your eyes looking at the horizon. 2. Stand up more erect. Try arching your back toward the boat. 3. Do not pick your foot up too high.*
Problem: *Can not keep the foot up. Constantly falling back down onto it.*
Diagnosis: *1. Lifting the foot up to the side. Pick it straight up keeping it close to your supporting leg. 2. Not shifting your body weight directly over your foot. 3. Start with your feet closer together.*

Backward Toehold

Skimming across the water backward on one foot with your arms free is a terrific sensation, and though it looks difficult, the backward toehold is a very relaxing and stable position. But before attempting the backward toehold, you should be very stable on one foot. The backward toehold handle is slightly longer than the forward toehold handle. It should be long enough so that you can comfortably regain the handle. Because the handle is behind you, you will have to find the strap by feel. A spreader bar in front of the toe strap will make the strap easier to locate.

1. Speed: Backward one-foot speed.
2. Assume backward one-foot position with eyes looking at the horizon and handle in the small of your back. Keep a slight bend in the skiing leg.
3. Keep your hips and shoulders level and be careful to maintain your balance as you slowly place your foot in the strap.
4. Slowly transfer the pull from your hands to your feet.
5. Use your arms for balance.

KEY: BALANCE!

Problem/Diagnosis

Problem: *Strap keeps slipping off.*
Diagnosis: *Your foot is not all the way in the strap. Place the strap high on your foot, and curl your toes and foot back toward your shin.*
Problem: *Falling over to the side.*
Diagnosis: *1. Weight is not centered over your supporting foot. 2. Your shoulders and hips are not level. Keep your body squarely facing backward. 3. Ski leg is too straight.*

Maintain an upright stance with knees close together.

180 And 360 Degree Turns

Turns are the most challenging of tricks, and they require the most technique of all barefoot maneuvers. Tournament trick runs now resemble those on skis consisting of 360's, 540's, wake turns, line turns, and toe turns!

Previous trick skiing or shoe skiing experience will be helpful since the fundamentals for barefoot turns are very much the same. The main difference in barefoot turns is that "unweighting" is more important than when on skis. Concentrate on these fundamentals:

1. Bring your free hand around quickly to the handle, keeping it close to your body. This will help your turn as well as increase the chances of pulling out of an imperfect turn.

2. Keep your eyes looking at the horizon. Do not look down, particularly when backward.

3. Rotate on your axis on an imaginary line through your head, shoulders, hips, and feet. Do not change the angle of your axis during a turn, i.e. do not lean any further away from the boat than the angle at which you begin your turn.

4. Always concentrate on doing your tricks feet-to-feet. This will make them much more enjoyable and easier, as well as speeding up your run in competition.

Slowly place your foot into the toestrap, being careful to maintain your balance.

Slowly release your grasp and keep an upright stance.

Barefooting 83

TRICKS

Back-To-Front

The back-to-front can be performed consistently at a wide range of speeds and water conditions, and therefore, highlights the finish of the backward barefoot act in many ski shows. There are two different techniques used, but I will describe the one which works best for me. It requires a definite "hop," allowing the feet to turn off the water. Timing the hop and turn is the critical part of the back-to-front.

1. Assume a comfortable, upright stance with shoulders, hips, and feet in line. The knees should be bent with feet 1 to 2 feet apart.

2. Hop up off the water by springing with the knees and then retracting your knees to pick your feet up off the water.

3. As you lift your feet, initiate the turn by simultaneously letting go with one hand and turning your head.

4. Grasp the handle in the front position and land softly by bending the knees.

Problem/Diagnosis

Problem: *Feet are catching the water and tripping you when starting the turn.*
Diagnosis: 1. Not unweighting enough, pick your feet up off the water more. 2. Starting your turn before feet are unweighted. 3. Feet too wide.

Problem: *Landing forward but getting pulled over.*
Diagnosis: 1. Arms are outstretched. Keep them in close during the turn. 2. Landing stiff-legged. Bend in the knees upon landing.

Problem: *Cannot grab the handle with free hand when forward.*
Diagnosis: 1. Handle is too far from body. Pull it in throughout the turn. 2. Free arm in not coming around quick enough.

Problem: *Sitting back on your bottom when forward:*
Diagnosis: 1. You are not keeping on your axis. Do not lean away too much. 2. You are starting and turning bent at the waist too much.

Bend your knees when preparing to spring up. Keep your feet one to two feet apart.

Hop up off the water. Let go with one hand and lead the turn with your head.

TIP

"There are several ways to do back-to-fronts. I'll describe the easiest way to learn it. The beginning position is important:

1. Arms out so that the pull is coming from your shoulders;

2. Feet together, the closer the better (ankle bones touching). That is the safest way to not hurt your knees.

3. Knees bent and slightly leaning away at the waist.

"To do the turn to the right, slowly let the pull go to your right hand. Keep your legs in one position as if they were on one wide ski. Let go with the left hand and the rope will automatically pull you around. As you come around, pull the handle in to your hips. As you come forward, bend your knees a little and spread your feet.

"This technique develops the technique needed for the more advanced style back-to-front. This advanced style is executed the same way except you upweight and time it so that the handle pulls you around at the peak of the unweight.

"I think it is important that you not keep the handle all the way in, because then it can only go out. With it out you can use it more effectively."
Ron Scarpa

"Start with a very narrow stance and shift 90% of your weight to your strong foot. Don't try to turn—just let go with one hand (opposite the foot your standing on) and it will turn you right around. You'll pivot on your weighted foot and your unweighted foot will swing underneath you.

"There are only three problems you can have when you're doing this:

1. You'll put your unweighted foot down too soon, stopping your turn;

2. You'll be pulled out the front because of not keeping your shoulders back; and

3. You'll fall off axis because your arms are out. Pull the handle in during the turn and lean to compensate for the direction your falling off axis."
Mike Seipel

Keep the handle in close and rotate on your axis.

Grasp the handle in the front position and land softly by bending the knees.

TRICKS

Front-To-Back

For a long time the front-to-back was thought to be next to impossible even though a few barefooters such as Don Thompson, Buster McCalla, and Randy Rabe were making them back in the early sixties. Its development has revolutionized barefooting as much as the reverse toeturn has revolutionized trick skiing. At the 1978 National and World Barefoot tournaments, Mike Botti demonstrated how effortlessly the front-to-back can be done. Since that time many other people have learned it, although it is still a tough trick to perform consistently.

Some of the falls you will encounter when learning the front-to-back will be the most painful you will ever experience. For some reason the whiplash is much more severe than regular backward falls. In fact, many people, including myself, have had to completely stop backward barefooting for a while because of their neck becoming so tender.

Some people find it helpful to use a neck collar to reduce the whiplash. You can also reduce the number of unnecessary falls by 1) practicing only in good conditions, i.e. calm water, correct speed, good driver; 2) rehearsing it on land before taking to the water; 3) visualizing yourself doing it and skiing away; and 4) having an observer watch and instruct.

The front-to-back is done with the feet remaining on the water, though unweighted. The positioning of the feet varies with every individual. For a turn to the left, some will step around, pivoting on the left foot, while others step underneath, pivoting on their right. I recommend that you do not concentrate on pivoting on a foot, but rather concentrate on switching places with feet. That is essentially swiveling on a point directly beneath you. The following steps will help you learn this trick.

1. Speed: Backward one-foot speed or slightly slower.
2. Feet fairly narrow.
3. Crouch very low keeping torso erect.
4. "Up-weight" by straightening your legs. Do not jump!
5. Begin your turn as you are rising.
6. Swivel your feet and body and pull the handle in as you turn.

Crouch low with a narrow stance.

7. Grasp handle and spread feet to normal backward stance.
8. Use your knees as shock absorbers when settling on the water.

Problem/Diagnosis

Problem: *Not even close.*
Diagnosis: *1. Throwing the turn too hard. You're thinking it's too difficult. Turn gently as though you were on skis. 2. Improper unweighting and turning. Remember, crouch low and begin turning as you are rising. 3. Catching a foot early in the turn is caused by turning too soon or beginning too far forward.*
Problem: *Constantly falling down onto chest.*
Diagnosis: *1. Dropping a shoulder and shifting your axis away from the the boat too much. Keep your head up and shoulders level as you turn. 2. Looking down at the water rather than at the horizon.*
Problem: *Constantly catching a heel backward:*
Diagnosis: *1. Landing stiff-legged. Bend at knees. 2. Your feet are not squarely reaching the backward position, i.e. one foot is behind the other. Concentrate on attaining a square backward barefoot position. Bringing the handle in to the middle of your back will help.*

Begin the turn as you rise.

Swivel your feet and body and pull the handle in as you turn.

Stay on your axis and keep your eyes on the horizon.

Concentrate on finishing in a solid and square backward position.

TRICKS

TIP

"The front-to-back is the most difficult trick to learn. Practicing on shoe skis is important to develop the technique without hard 35-40 mph falls.

"There are three ingredients to the turn which should be practiced on shoe skis: a smooth unweight, the turn, and grabbing the handle.

"There are many different styles of turning and they all work. How you turn is not that important. Only that you have unweighted and finished square and with both hands on the handle.

"Begin learning it on shoe skis at 25 mph. When you're comfortable, begin slowing the boat speed down to as slow as 15 mph. The increased drag will require you to have a definite unweight, and it will be very similar to doing it on barefeet. Once you can do this, do the same thing on your feet at a comfortable front barefoot speed." **Mike Seipel**

"Start with you weight centered over your feet and arms out slightly. Begin with a slight upweight. As you're upweighting, pull the handle in to your hip. This helps to turn you.

"I recommend either switching your feet (rotating on a point between your feet) or stepping over (pivoting on the left foot if turning to the left). Keep your feet fairly close throughout the turn, and land in a stable backward position, whatever position is best for you."

Ron Scarpa

360-Degree Turn

The 360 is not difficult if you do very good front-to-backs and back-to-fronts. A good smooth front-to-back is essential for consistent 360's. You must complete the front-to-back so that you are in the proper position to go right into a back-to-front without any hesitation. If you can do that, it is just a matter of putting the two together into one fluid movement.

This can be done upweighting each 180, or by pivoting the back-to-front. Either method works fine, but strive to stay on axis for a smooth, clean and fun turn.

Turning the front-to-back portion of the turn slowly rather than snapping it can help prevent hesitating in the back position. This allows you more time to grip the handle and start the back-to-front.

It is important to keep your feet close together throughout the turn. Don't let them spread when you reach the back position as might be the tendency for regular front-to-backs.

There can, of course, be no delay in getting the handle in the back position. Any delay will cause you to hesitate the turn.

Finally, as you develop more and more the feel of your feet on the water, it will become second nature for you to know how much unweight and what foot positioning is needed to prevent catching.

TIP

"If you're not a very confident skier, there's no point in even attempting it. If you don't have complete control over your front-to-back and back-to-fronts, don't even waste your time. If your turns are great, then a 360 should be absolutely no problem. The difficulty for most people is that you have to be able to do your reverse back-to-front.

"Do the same thing you would do on a front-to-back, but don't upweight so much that you get air under both feet. You want your feet to stay on the water.

Barefooting 89

TRICKS

"Don't pull in so hard on the handle that you get slack—keep a tight rope. Also, the handle should be pulled in close enough so that you have good handle control. If it gets too far out, it will pull you over when you come around forward." **Ron Scarpa**

"The key to a good feet-to-feet 360 is a smooth front-to-back. When you get the handle in the back position, that's your cue to come forward. If you don't get the handle right away, you'll do a quick front-to-back and back-to-front, but not a 360." **Mike Seipel**

360 Back-To-Back

TIP

"To do a legitimate back-to-back, you can't unweight on the front-to-back. It requires a slow back-to-front, then as soon as you can, even before you get forward, grab the handle with the other hand. Pull in on the handle to keep rotating and push hard forward on your feet. You basically pivot the whole turn on one foot, the left foot if turning to the left." **Mike Seipel**

"Start upright with your feet close together. I shift the handle to the right to prepare for a turn to the right. It is important to pull in on the handle as you come to the front position. If the handle is out, it will stop your rotation. You must stay over your feet - you can't lean away too far on this trick. And again, keep your feet close together so they slide around nicely." **Ron Scarpa**

540

TIP

"To do a 540 you must be able to do a beautifully clean 360 finishing over your feet with the handle in tight, then go right into the front-to-back. 540's are hardly unweighted at all, you can actually feel your feet on the water as you're turning. You have to learn to push your feet to the front so they don't catch. This requires a feel of your feet on the water which is developed only after much experience, and only very few of the top barefooters have it. These tricks are only for super good barefooters to try." **Ron Scarpa**

"All I think about on a back-to-front 540 is doing a smooth back-to-back 360, then as soon as I grab the handle I go right into a back-to-front. Or a smooth front-to-front 360 and as soon as I grab the handle I do a front-to-back for a front-to-back 540. There is no unweight involved. It is more of a pivot on one foot keeping the foot pushed out in front of the handle." **Mike Seipel**

Wake Turns

Once you master surface turns, wake turns should not pose much of a problem. Use the same basic principles as surface turns with the following considerations: drift toward the wake (do not cut), do not spring too hard — let the wake do the work for you, land softly bending the knees.

Generally, front-to-backs are done from inside to outside the wake and back-to-fronts outside to inside.

The critical part of a wake turn is timing your spring and turn off the crest of the wake. Beginning too early is the common mistake. This will cause your feet to catch and trip you up.

Wake back-to-fronts are the easiest wake turns. The most difficult part of this is being able to see the wake, since you are facing backward. This requires you to develop a feel for the wake.

It is easier to time your spring on wake front-to-backs, but the landing is more difficult. Therefore do not spring too high. That will only make the landing more difficult.

Drift toward the wake.

Spring off the top of the wake.

Land softly by bending your knees.

Timing the spring is done mostly by feel in the back position.

Lift your feet up for extra height.

Land with knees bent and handle in.

Barefooting **91**

TRICKS

Back-To-Front-Stepover

This is a very easy trick which, unfortunately, is almost always performed sloppily. Although it can be performed feet-to-feet, it is more difficult and most barefooters prefer not to do it. Quite a few knee injuries have resulted from the step-over, so use caution and good judgment.

Place the handle between the legs by letting go with one hand and turning the handle down so that it is vertical and in the center of your back. Then reach between your legs to grasp it with your free hand. Once stable, place the free hand on the handle as well.

1. Speed: Backward one-foot speed.
2. Feet close together.
3. Lean away and roll to front position swinging leg over rope.
4. Hang on and stand up onto your feet.

The back-to-front stepover, or "line front" violates several of the basic fundamentals of proper tricking. First, you lean further away from the boat, as you turn, going for a three-point landing. Second, you remain bent at the waist throughout the turn rather than straight.

TIP

"The line front is the easiest trick in the book. You don't have to be able to do it on shoe skis or trick skis. All you need to be able to do is do it on the living room carpet! Practice the whole thing on land, including passing the handle. Once you get the handle between your legs, arch your shoulders up and bend your knees. Then just swing your leg over the rope while rolling over to your butt and back."

The Powells

"To do this trick feet-to-feet it should first be learned on shoe skis.

"First, place the handle between your legs and lift up one foot as high as the rope or actually resting on the rope. Then give a slight unweight to hop forward and land on both feet. Once you can do this consistently, blend the two movements into one so that lifting the leg actually becomes part of the unweighting."

Mike Seipel

The "roll over, sit down, stand up" style stepover.

The feet-to-feet style stepover.

Barefooting **93**

TRICKS

Front-To-Back-Stepover

The front-to-back step-over has been one of the most difficult tricks, and the falls from it can be terrible. Therefore only the most experienced barefooter should attempt it.

TIP

"This trick was originally incredibly difficult, but refined technique has made it much easier, although it is still very difficult. The easiest way to learn it is to do a one foot and place the other foot on the line. When you decide to turn, just set the foot down backward. This rotates you right around. Once you can do this conveniently, put it all into one smooth movement." **Mike Seipel**

"You first need to be able to do a toe-back or one foot front-to-back before attempting this trick. Start with your feet slightly narrower than shoulder width apart and the handle straight up and down.

"Upweight as you would for a one foot front-to-back, but as you begin, also start a smooth yet hard downward pull of the handle toward your skiing knee. This gets the rope low so your leg can go over it easily. Simultaneously bring your knee up and over the rope. I find letting go with one hand half way through the turns gives me better balance.

"Slowly set your foot onto the water once the leg is over the line and you're backward on one foot.

"It is important to concentrate on keeping your eyes at the horizon and back erect because the pull of the rope will tend to pull you down through your legs." **Rick Powell**

Start crouched with a narrow stance and the handle straight up and down.

Pull the handle down while lifting your knee over the line.

Gently set your foot on the water.

94 Barefooting

Toehold Front-To-Back

The toe front-to-back is one of the most enjoyable tricks to do. When executed properly it is really quite easy and effortless. You can upweight it slightly or just snap it around. Many people swing their arms quite a bit to help turn them. I prefer swinging the arms as little as possible, and instead initiating the turn with the hips.

1. Begin in a comfortable front toe position with your torso erect.
2. Crouch down by bending your skiing leg.
3. Upweight and turn just like a front-to-back.
4. Keep your head up and torso erect to stay on axis.
5. The skiing knee should be bent as your weight settles onto it.

In tournament competition you'll see toe front-to-backs with the person finishing the trick bent over at the waist and butt sometimes higher than their head! Just because top competitors do it that way doesn't mean you should. They do it so that they are low to the water ready to roll to their butt for a toe-back-toe-front.

TIP

"The toe front-to-back is another trick which is good to first learn on shoe skis. When trying it barefooted you need to have a solid back toehold at front toehold speed.

"If you are turning to the left, start with your right arm to the side and your left arm in front so that you can initiate the turn with your arms and upper body. They will then already be three-quarters of the way turned before you turn your foot.

"There is a very small unweight needed as you snap your foot around, but because the foot is snapped around so quickly, the unweight really isn't that crucial."

Mike Seipel

"The trick to the toe back is to practice it in your living room with your foot on the corner of a chair. Learn to turn without moving your foot on the chair. The turn is initiated with the shoulders and upper body. Don't bend at the waist—keep an upright position. No upweight is required, and don't snap the turn too quickly."

The Powells

Crouch down, bending your skiing leg.

Unweight and turn just as you would in a front-to-back.

Keep your head up and torso erect to stay on your axis.

TRICKS

Toehold Back-To-Front

Like the back-to-front step-over, the "toe front" is generally performed very sloppily by merely rolling over on to your butt from the backward toe position, and then doing a forward toe stand-up. Thus, if you cannot do a forward toe stand-up, learn that first.

Keep your skiing leg fairly straight and lean away far from the boat, then spin to your butt. Leaning away gets you low to the water so you don't have as far to fall to the water.

One-Foot Turns

TIP

"There are three keys to one-foot turns.

1. There is much more drag so you need to concentrate on keeping the handle in.

2. The foot needs to be kept directly underneath the rope. If it gets out to the side just a little bit, it will make you put the other foot down.

3. Keep the foot pushed out in front of you. Unweight the front-to-back by pushing the foot forward, not down. The back-to-front doesn't need any unweight at all, but bend the knee and sit low when you come forward."

Mike Seipel

NOTE: One foot turns can be executed on either foot in either direction.

Crouch low.

Roll to the front.

Proceed as you would for a front toe standup.

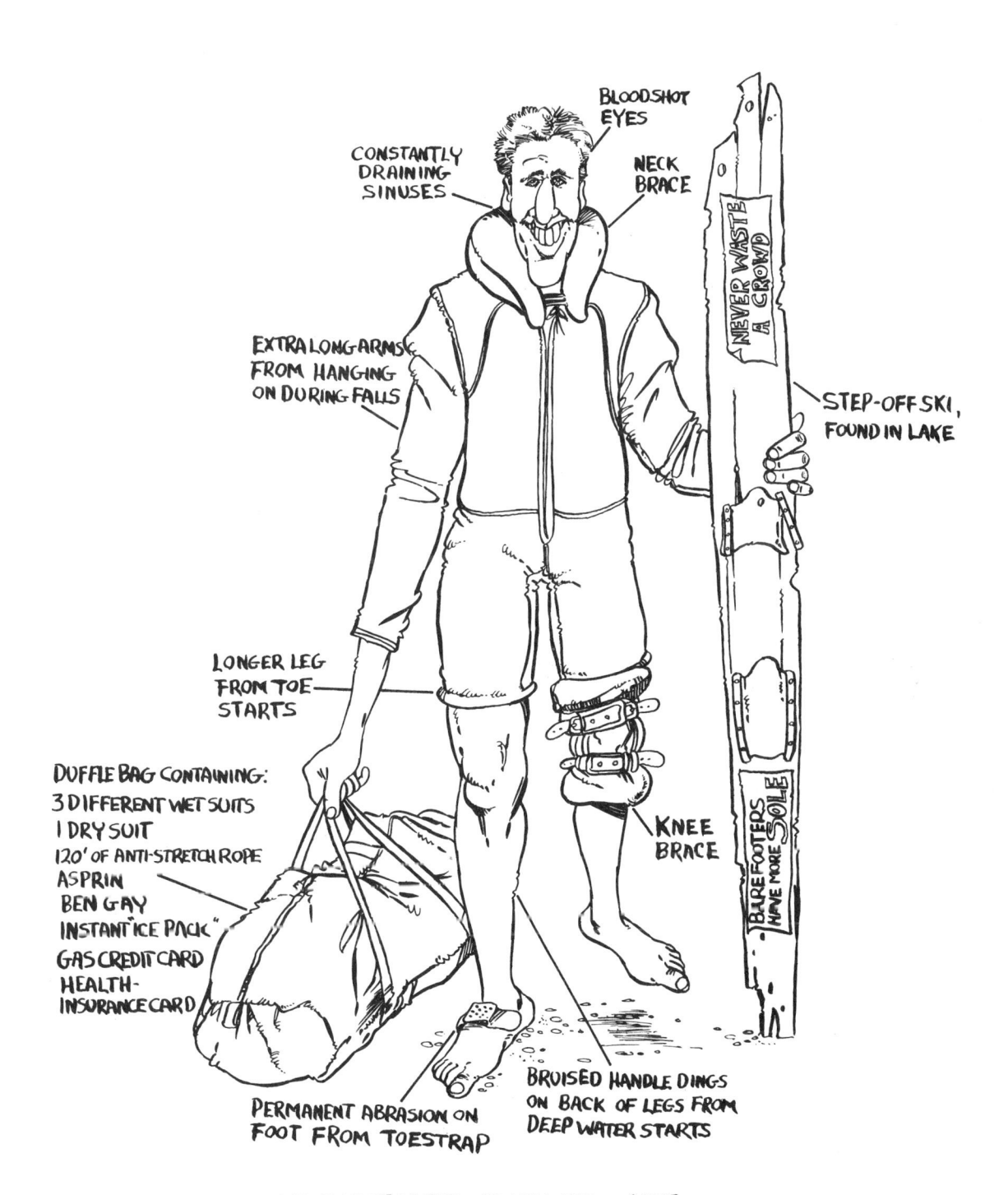

THE BAREFOOTER EXTRAORDINAIRE

TRICKS

98 Barefooting

Barefooting 99

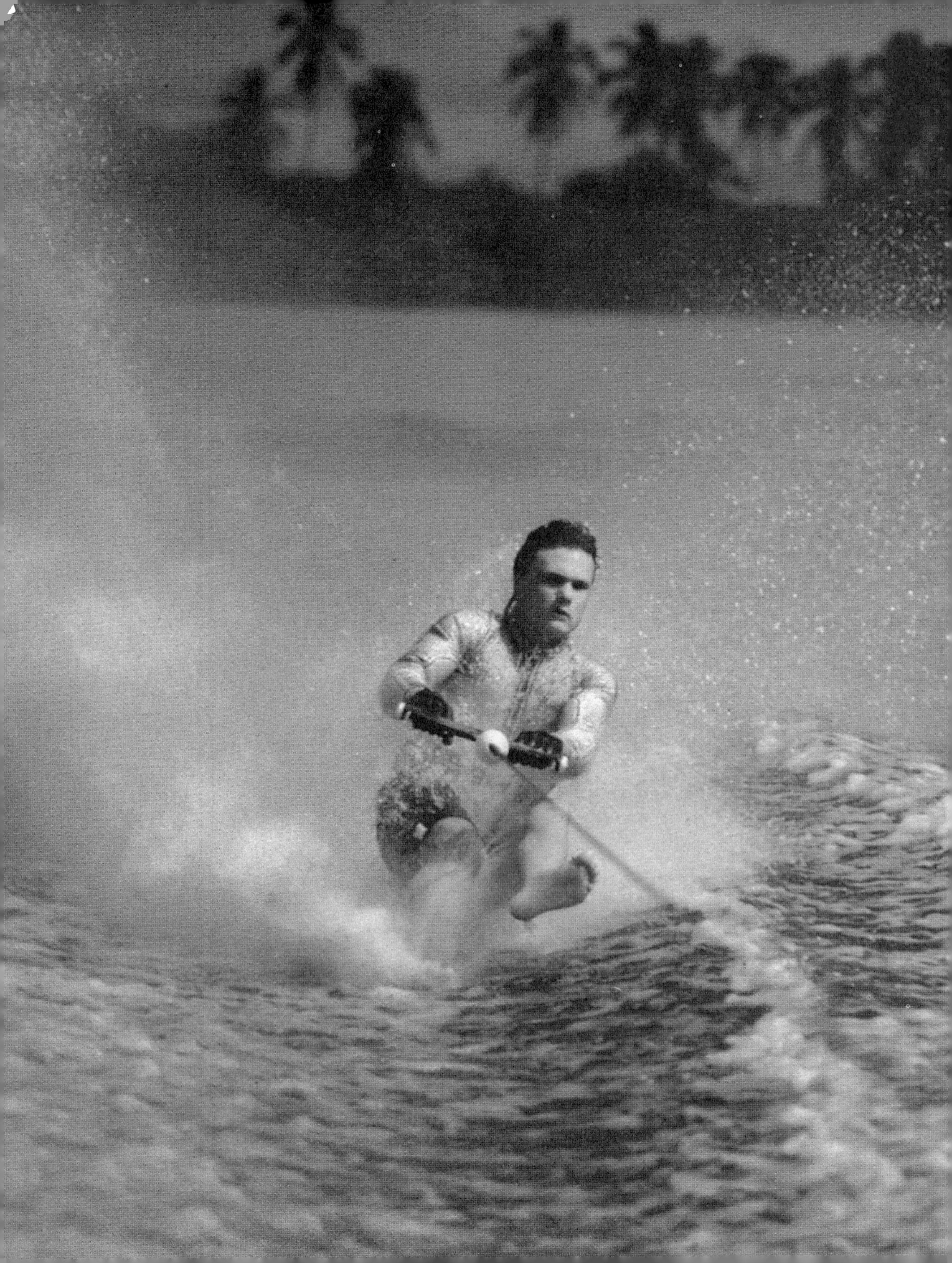

STEERING AND WAKE SLALOM

Forward Steering

The ability to steer and cross the wake is important for maximum enjoyment of the sport and it is the first big challenge the beginning barefooter will encounter.

Shoe ski or even trick ski experience will help here because the technique is essentially the same. The key is to cut or "edge" with the outside foot. It's called "edging" because you use the edges of your feet (or skis). This is done primarily with the outside foot.

To steer to the right, turn your feet, knees, hips, and shoulders to the right slightly and place more pressure or weight on the left foot by shifting your body and handle over to that foot. Your right foot can be edging too, but it won't have the same amount of drive as the more weighted left foot.

Many people barefoot with too wide of a stance, and this really hampers them. A wide stance prevents you from getting your weight over your outside cutting foot as well as causing the inside foot to work against you. A narrower than normal stance is best for good steering.

The harder and quicker you want to cut, the more weight you place on the outside foot.

Top tournament footers will verify that to gain maximum speed on a cut, their weight is solely (so to speak) on the one foot. Therefore, effective steering and cutting requires increased boat speed. In fact, good forward one-foot wake slalomers ask for the highest speeds of anyone in tournaments!

Advanced water ski jumpers use this same technique on their counter cut. They get a more powerful edge and dig by picking up the inside ski.

So much for steering technique. Let's go for the wake.

Many novices have the misconception that you step over the wake, picking the first foot up and over, then the second foot. All wrong! Start a few feet away from the wake to get your momentum going and drive all the way through the wake with the outside foot (left foot if going to the right.) The only change in body position is to lean back slightly

Mike Seipel digs in hard on a one foot wake slalom cut.

Steer by turning your feet, knees, hips, and shoulders and edging with the outside foot.

Barefooting 101

STEERING AND WAKE SLALOM

more to get more angle on your feet (getting the toes higher) so that you don't catch a toe.

Again it is important to keep a narrow stance. With a wide stance you won't be digging well with the outside foot, and it is likely that that foot will get hung up on the wake resulting in either the splits or catching a toe.

Of course you will also need to maintain a good barefoot stance through this steering and wake crossing, i.e., the "sitting-in-a-chair" position with knees bent, shoulders slightly behind the hips, and arms slightly bent with the handle held low.

Backward Steering

Backward steering and wake crossing is accomplished by edging exclusively with the outside foot. The inside foot is unweighted and just coasts across the surface of the water.

It is also important to shift your body and handle over the cutting foot. Leaning well away from the boat will help prevent catching a heel as well as increasing your "dig."

Backward cutting differs from forward in that you don't turn your hips and shoulders as much and your stance is not as narrow. It might even be wider than your normal backward stance.

Here is a recap of the steering and wake crossing technique:

1. Steer mainly with the outside foot.

2. Turn the feet, knees, hips, and shoulders in the direction you wish to go (mainly for forward).

3. Apply pressure to the outside cutting foot by shifting your body and handle over the foot.

4.. Lean away from the boat slightly more than normal to prevent catching a toe.

Start cutting about three to five feet from it.

Drive all the way across with your outside foot.

102 Barefooting

Competitive Wake Slalom

Competitive wake crossing consists of two fifteen second passes in which the contestant crosses the wake completely from one side to the other as many times as he can. The contestant has the option of going forward or backward, on one foot or two. He may also have a combination of one foot and two foot crossings. Often a skier will have a strong one foot crossing in only one direction, therefore he will do one foot crossings in one direction, returning in the opposite direction on two feet.

The most number of wake crossings in each fifteen second pass is either nine front one-foot crossings or 11 backward one-foot.

Forward Crossings

Forward two-feet crossings are the easiest of the four types of crossings. Attempt them at your normal one-footing speed. Get a good start by beginning three to five feet outside the wake and charging at it. Continue to drive all the way across the wake with your outside foot. Sit back well enough to keep your toes from catching but not so far that you bog in. Be careful that your inside foot (right foot if you're going from left to right) doesn't get behind you and trip up. Keep it in front of you by straightening it a little more than the outside leg. Be sure you keep your knees bent, using the knees as shock absorbers over the wakes.

The technique is the same for one-foot crossings. One foots require the driving foot to be directly underneath you.

Sit back slightly so that your toes don't catch.

Use the knees as shock absorbers over the wakes.

Barefooting 103

STEERING AND WAKE SLALOM

Problem/Diagnosis

Problem: *Constantly catching your toes.*
Diagnosis: *1. You are too far forward with feet too level. Sit back a bit more, banking your feet.*
2. Speed too slow.
Problem: *Getting caught in the wake and losing momentum.*
Diagnosis: *1. Not building enough momentum before the wake. 2. You are chickening-out and not continuing to drive through the wake. 3. Speed too slow.*

TIP

"Begin by getting into the strongest forward barefoot position you can. This position is slightly different for everybody, so get in the position strongest for you.

1. Bring your feet close together, then put your outside foot directly underneath the rope.
2. Turn your foot in the direction you want to cut.
3. Push your foot toward the boat by leaning back slightly. Keep your skiing leg bent.

"Start far enough away from the wake so that you build enough momentum to keep you from getting caught on the crest of the wake.

"As you progressively cut harder and put more and more pressure on the outside foot, you'll naturally move right into one foot crossings. The technique is essentially the same."

Mike Seipel

Pick your foot up after establishing your cut to the wake.

Pick the foot up directly in front of you, not to the side.

104 Barefooting

"**1.** Try to keep your shoulders nearly level when doing forward one foot wake slalom.
2. Pick the foot up straight in front of you, not to the side.
3. Turn your shoulders, hips and foot in the direction you want to go, and look in that direction.
4. The body position is the basic sitting-in-a-chair position with the foot in front of the knee, knees in front of hips, and hips in front of shoulders, and arms out.
5. The foot on the water is fairly flat with the toes curled up. Don't dig your heel in too hard and be aware of where the water is hitting your foot.
6. Both legs are bent.
7. The handle is held over the right hip if going to the left.
8. When reversing the direction of the cut outside the wake, it is crucial to move the handle from one hip to the other." **Ron Scarpa**

Keep your skiing foot directly underneath the rope.

Maintain a strong sitting-in-the-chair position.

Barefooting 105

STEERING AND WAKE SLALOM

Backward Crossings

Backward crossings can be faster than forward crossings. When backward barefooting you have a wider part of your foot in the water enabling you to "edge" or cut more effectively. The disadvantage of the backward crossing is that you can't see where you are and must learn to "feel" the wake as you cross it.

The body position for backward wake crossing is one with the shoulders, hips, and feet almost in a straight line. Lean away from the boat at about a 45 degree angle with the feet about shoulder width apart. Keep your eyes at the horizon for good balance, and your arms can be fairly straight with the handle on your buttocks. Do not turn your body as in front wake slalom, turn only your foot.

Steering is done totally with the foot opposite the direction you wish to travel. Transfer more weight to the foot and turn it in the direction you wish to go. During rapid wake crossings all your weight will be on your outside foot. When making the transition outside the wake, the key is to shift your weight quickly over the other foot. Keeping your feet fairly close will help you to do this.

The technique for one-foot crossings is the same, it is just more critical to have your driving foot directly underneath you.

Turn your cutting foot toward the wake and place more weight on it.

The cutting foot is placed underneath the rope.

Problem/Diagnosis

Problem: *Not gaining speed across the wake.*
Diagnosis: 1. Not applying enough pressure to the driving foot. Bring it directly underneath you. 2. Foot is not turned toward the direction you are turning.
Problem: *Slow transition outside the wake.*
Diagnosis:
1. Not shifting your weight quickly. 2. Feet are too wide. 3. Putting your foot down too wide on one-foot tricks.
Problem: *Catching heels often.*
Diagnosis: 1. You're not leaning away far enough. 2. You're bent at the waist too much.
Problem: *Dropping off the wake.*
Diagnosis: 1. Not leaning away enough. 2. Not driving all the way through the wake.
Problem: *Setting your foot down too early on one-foot tricks.*
Diagnosis: 1. Your foot is not directly underneath you.

Most of your weight is on the cutting foot.

Feel for the wake to know when you're over it.

Barefooting 107

STEERING AND WAKE SLALOM

TIP

"The basic technique for backward crossing is the same as forward crossing except the feet are wider—a comfortable stance about shoulder width apart. The body is leaning away and straight with shoulders, hips and feet in a line; not bent over at the waist.

"To cut across the wake do three things:

1. Bring your outside foot underneath the rope.
2. Push it toward the boat by leaning away slightly
3. Turn it in the direction you want to go.

"To keep from jumping off the second wake, do not bend your knee as you might think. Keep your leg straight and drive all the way through both wakes. This is the key to fast wakes. Cut with full power through both wakes, and then make the transition." **Mike Seipel**

"**1.** Start in a good solid back barefoot position with feet just wider than shoulder width apart. Knees should have a natural bend in them; not locked out straight. Arms are straight and at your sides. Bending at the waist is fine, but keep your eyes at the horizon.
2. Turn the foot and cut just like when you are going forward. Move the handle over the foot you're standing on.
3. For one-foot, start toward the wake with 80 percent of your weight on the outside foot, then just before the wake pick up your foot.
4. Anticipate the wake and watch for it with your peripheral vision.
5. As your skiing foot is crossing the second crest you should already be bringing down the lifted foot." **Ron Scarpa**

Body position is the same as on two feet.

Anticipate the wake and watch for it with your peripheral vision.

Keep your foot underneath the rope.

Landing on both feet can help prevent catching a heel.

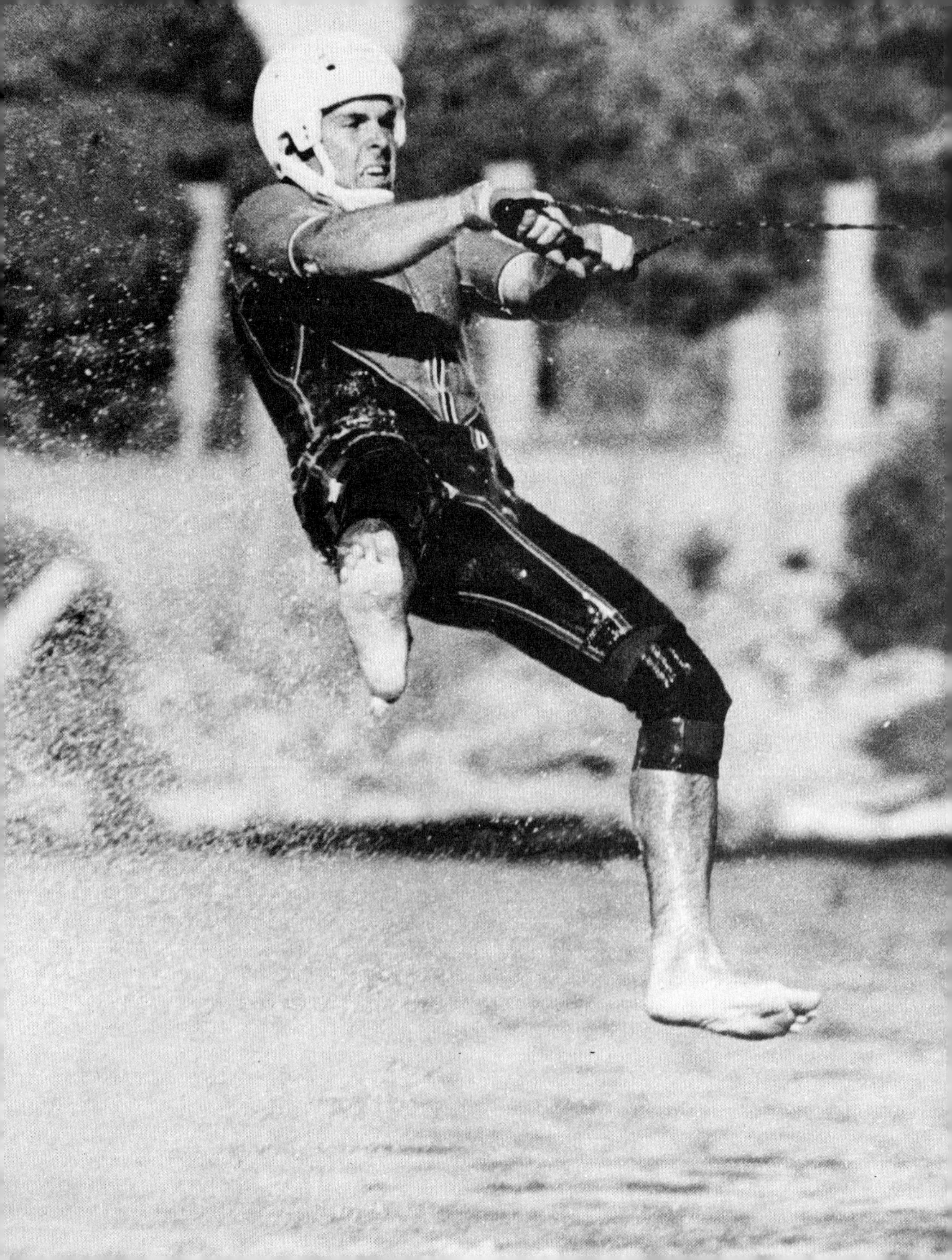

JUMPING

Jumping is the most dangerous and controversial of all barefoot events. The ramp's surface is extremely slippery and if you approach it in the normal "leaning back" barefoot position, your feet will slip out and you will end up landing with your feet well above your head! Even Ron Scarpa slipped out so bad on his first attempt that he hit his butt *And head* on the ramp!

So to successfully complete a jump, you have to approach the ramp with your weight forward, increasing the chances of falling forward onto the ramp. Tragically, several barefooters have broken their necks from falls like this. Falls are not limited to novices either. Numerous champions have "eaten" the ramp, fortunately without serious injury. **I DISCOURAGE BAREFOOT JUMPING! I am including it only so that those of you determined to jump will learn it properly and with respect.**

While actual barefoot jumping is not very difficult, it should be approached with great discretion and common sense. Before even attempting to jump you should be an excellent forward barefooter. You should be very good at forward wake crossing, and should be able to do some intermediate tricks, like toeholds, which demonstrate balance and control on your feet.

Minimum equipment is a quality crash helmet, strong watertight shorts or wetsuit, and good flotation capable of floating you in the event of a fall. Never, never jump unless the water is perfectly calm.

ONLY ATTEMPT JUMPING WHEN THE WATER IS PERFECTLY CALM.

For your first attempt at the jump, have the boat go about one to two miles per hour faster than your normal two-foot speed so that your feet will plane easily over the surface. The boat should pass six to 10 feet away from the left side of the jump or far enough away so that the wake of the boat does not

Falls like these are what make barefooting controversial.

Ron Scarpa launches off the ramp.

Barefooting 111

JUMPING

disturb the jump before impact (why the left side and not the right as in classical skiing, I don't know). Some spray from the boat almost always hits the ramp though.

Hold the handle with both palms facing down. The baseball type grip can make you tilt a shoulder slightly off balance, and it is important to hit the jump perfectly square with shoulders level. Holding the handle vertically can also make it into a hammer that might be slammed into your abdominal area on a hard sit-down landing.

Crouch down low with your feet underneath you and about shoulder width apart or slightly narrower. Pull away from the wake lining up slightly to the right of the center of the jump. Just before hitting the jump, let up your pull or "cut" and distribute your weight evenly on both feet. Freeze, and hold this position over the jump. You will be pulled across the jump at a slight angle from right to left. If you continue your cut on the jump your feet will slip out to the side. Going over the jump happens quicker than you can blink an eye, and you will hardly realize you went over it.

Most jumpers have their feet slip out in front of them on their first jumps. "Crushing" or absorbing the ramp with your knees will help prevent this and make the landing easier. Raising the handle above your head is improper technique for water ski jumping, but can help you keep forward in the air during a barefoot jump.

Most people sit down on the landing. However, if properly executed you can land directly on your feet which is much cleaner, more enjoyable, and is actually easier than bouncing around on your rear and struggling to get to your feet. Whichever way you land, have the handle at waist level with your arms in when you hit the water. For a "feet-to-feet" landing, it is important to land soft by absorbing the impact in your knees. Regardless of how far you jump, it is always best to remain fairly upright so that you land on your feet first, letting them begin to absorb the landing, and then sit down to your butt if you need to.

112 Barefooting

This is why only very experienced barefooters should jump, and then only in perfectly calm water. Fortunately, this person was uninjured.

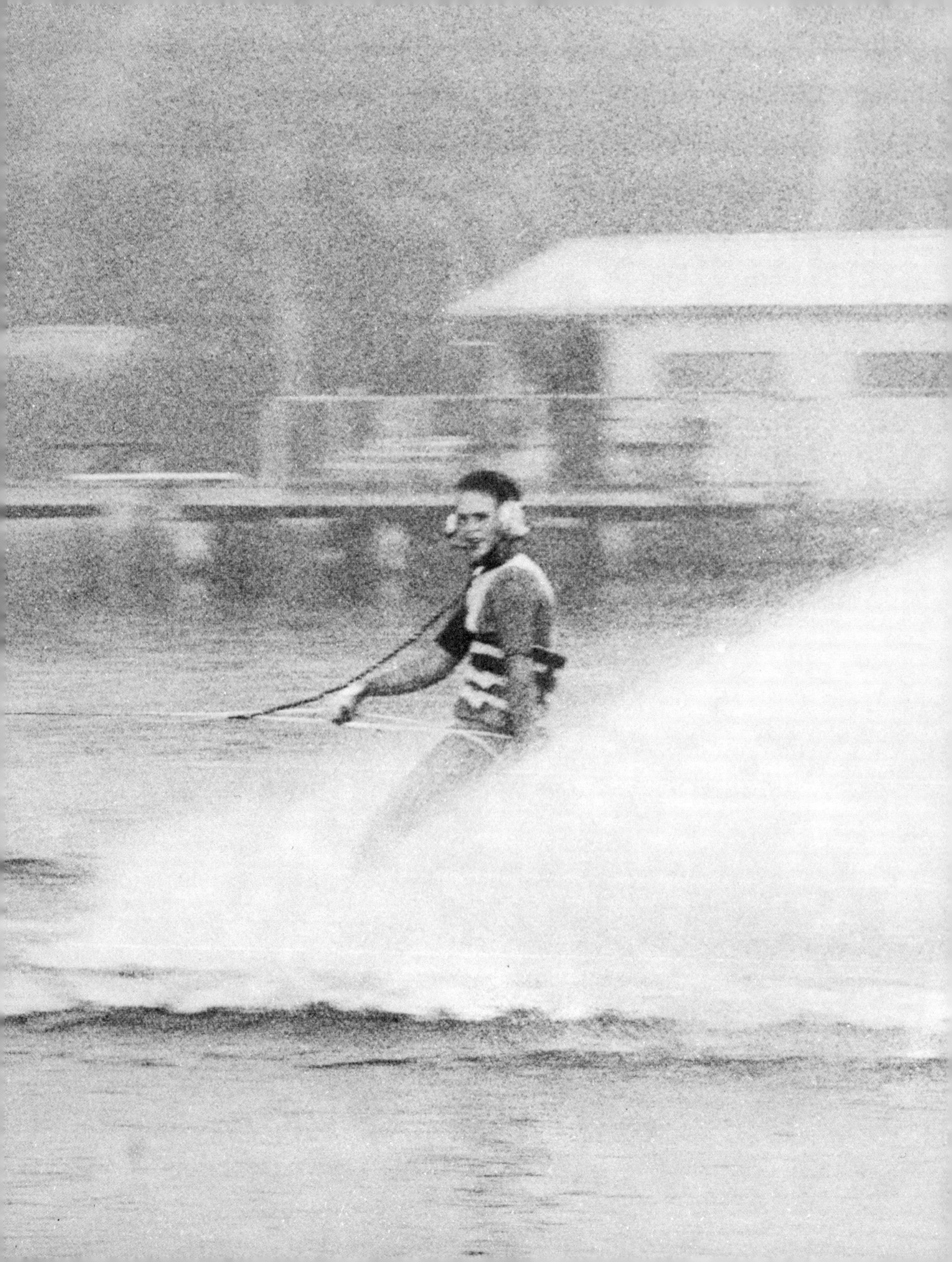

ENDURANCE

by Billy Nichols, world endurance record holder (2 hours, 42 minutes)

To start with, one must understand that endurance is a progression event, and it takes time on and off the water to build up your stamina. Both physical and mental conditioning are important.

If you are in good physical shape, there are still some things you can do. First, jogging is good for increasing overall stamina. Next, sit in the barefoot position on land while holding on to a ski rope with pulley and weight attached. This is a good way to develop the proper muscles for skiing without using all the gas.

One of the drawbacks for many skiers is sore feet. The only way I know how to get them tough is to barefoot on them. I try to ski in the prop wash a lot to toughen them. They may be a little sore the next day, but it might pay off later!

The only step that is left before getting down to skiing is your mental attitude. You need to be aggressive and confident. You should feel like all that dry land practice is finally going to be tested. Each time you practice endurance you should push yourself to stay up as long as possible. You may surprise yourself by going that extra minute or past that last big wave. This is a good way to build your confidence, which is so important.

I suggest you adjust the speed to your conditions (water, type of run you want to make, etc). For a long run on calm water, I suggest a very slow speed. Two to four m.p.h. below your normal speed is good, but have an understanding with the driver to speed up a predetermined amount for any rough water. For a rough water run, I suggest a mild speed drop of 1 to 2 m.p.h. so your feet will not mush into the waves.

The best boat trim that I have found for an outboard or inboard/outboard is down as far as it will go. This cuts down on the prop wash and makes the boat break the waves better.

Use your own discretion on the rope length. For most boats I prefer a fairly long rope, about 100 feet. This provides a good bit of room inside the wake, and gives you time to get ready for waves when you see the boat bounce.

Your signals with the boat driver should be predetermined and definite. Speeds should only be changed 1/2 to 1 m.p.h. Usually the skier can signal the driver which way he wants the boat to cut through a wave, i.e. straight on, parallel, etc. It is very helpful if the observer tells the skier how long he has been up if waves are ahead, boat speed, etc. All these signals should be discussed beforehand to avoid confusion.

Body position is important in endurance. You will need to pick several positions that are comfortable for you. For even slightly choppy water I suggest that you stay back with arms in and feet fairly wide. When you have a smooth patch of water it is best to stand up straighter with your feet closer together, enabling you to rest up for any rough water that might be ahead. A good position for resting in calm water is arms outstretched and body bent way over

The world record team (clockwise from top right): driver/father Perry Nichols, Billy Nichols, officiator Elmer Stailing, judge Tony Law.

Billy Nichols all "tricked-out" for his world record run. Headset was for communicating with the driver.

Barefooting **115**

ENDURANCE

at the waist. This will relax the arms and shoulders and relieve pressure on the back. But keep your feet in front of you and weight well back just in case you hit some waves.

Another way of relieving pressure on the back is by using a double-handle rope and holding the handles behind the back. However, this is only for long runs on calm water and should be considered very dangerous. The bridle should consist of two long ropes (approximately 10 feet) with small six-inch handles attached. A 14-inch ski handle placed about 26 inches from the two handles works well as a spreader bar. The handles are placed behind the back and gripped in one hand, while the spreader bar is held with the other hand for stability. This technique is recommended only for accomplished footers, and should be practiced on a ski before trying it barefooted.

When practicing wear a heavy, full-padded wet suit with flotation. But for tournaments, ski as lightweight as possible. Wet suit shorts and a ski jacket are fine.

Whenever you are practicing endurance, push yourself to the limit and then some. As the body builders say, "no pain, no gain"! So really push yourself and try your hardest, but keep safety in mind and always wear flotation.

The long and lonely ride.

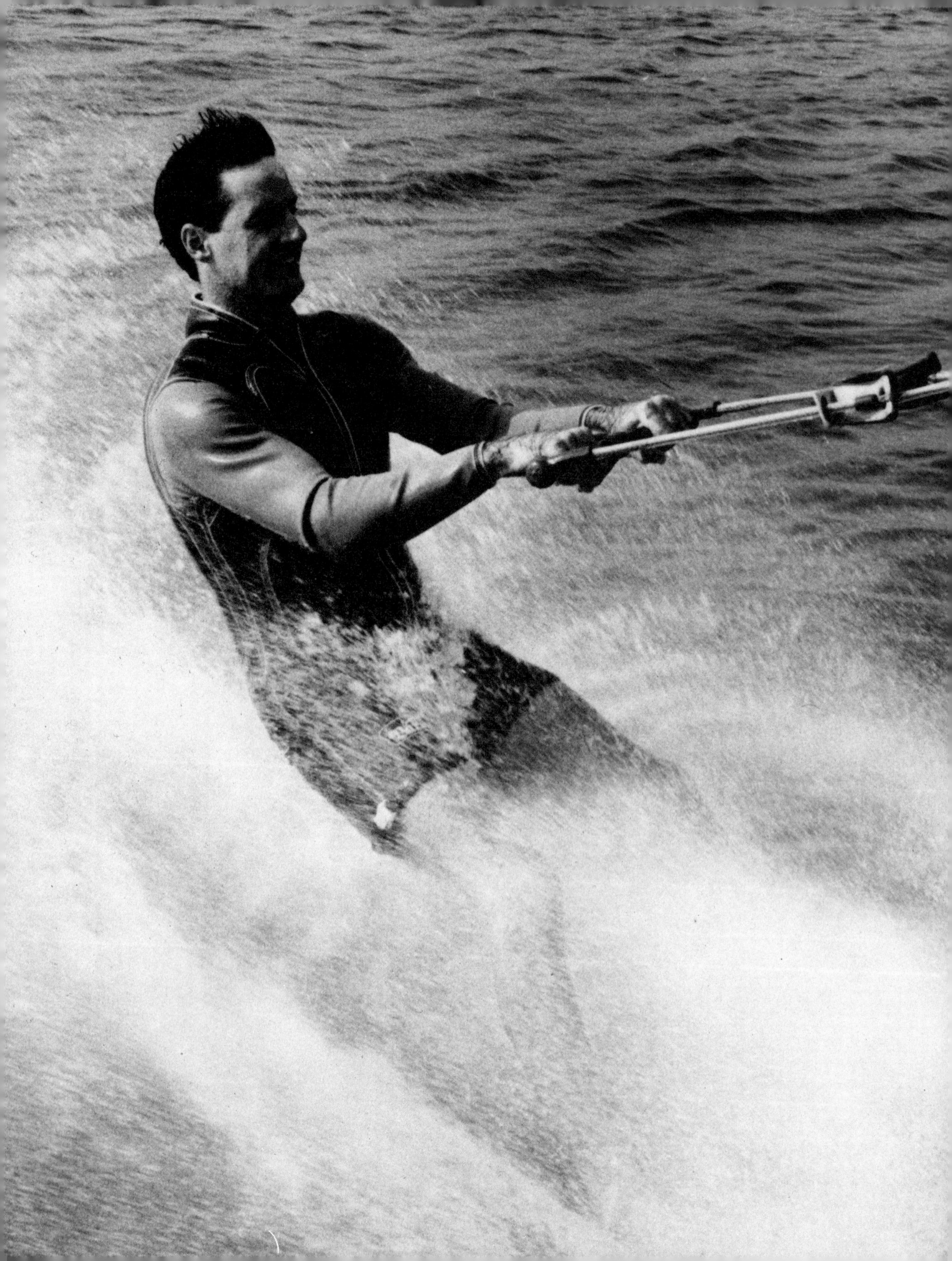

ROUGH WATER

Barefoot water skiing is a calm-water sport. However, every barefooter will inevitably encounter rough water. This makes barefooting much more difficult, but with proper technique you will often be able to keep from falling.

The boat speed should be just fast enough to keep your feet from penetrating too deeply into the waves, and no faster. A slower speed may allow your feet to mush into a wave, tripping you while too much speed will cause your feet to skip out of the water uncontrollably. Depending upon what your normal speed is, this "perfect" speed for rough water may be either slower or faster.

The two essential things for making it through rough water are leaning further away from the boat and increasing the angle of your feet in the water. This will feel like you are pushing your feet through the water rather than standing on top of them. They should be well in front of you.

Forward Stance

When leaning away from the boat, keep your torso leaning back slightly with your shoulders behind your hips and handle held at waist level and close to your body! Increasing the angle of your feet can be achieved by straightening your legs slightly and pushing your feet out in front of you.

In this position you will get a lot of spray in your face. Often you will not be able to see where you are going or be able to breathe. When barefooting through a series of waves you may have to take a big breath, lean back into the spray and hope your breath lasts longer than the waves! If it is consistently rough water, you may have to constantly hold your breath. When your air runs out you will have to risk leaning forward for an instant to catch a breath.

Backward Stance

Many good back-barefooters prefer attacking rough water backward rather than forward. It is a more relaxed stance and you do not have the problem of spray in the face. Also, because the part of the foot in the water is wider, you can go slower. Backward, you can pretty much utilize your whole foot, while in forward barefooting, as soon as the water rises above the ball of your foot it is "goodbye." However, it is very difficult to get off the ski backward in rough water, and you also have the problem of not being able to see the waves. The nice thing is that you can breath easily!

Basically all you do is spread your feet and lean away. You may even end up with your nose inches from the water! A slight bend at the waist may be helpful.

Keep your weight back and your feet well out in front of you.

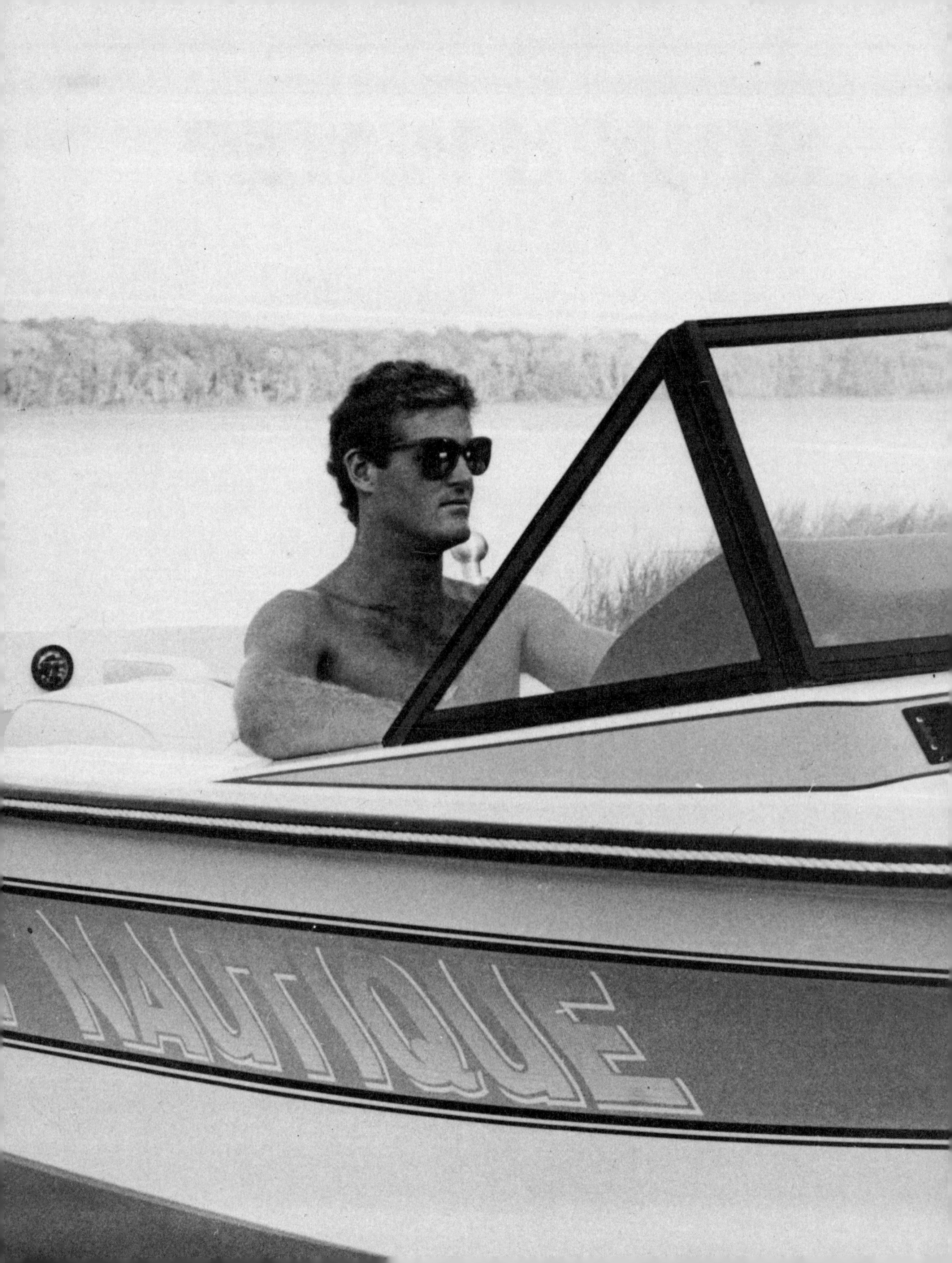
NAUTIQUE

BOAT DRIVING

It takes just as much concentration for the driver to drive well as it does for the skier to ski well. As a driver you need to constantly be aware of the skier, the boat speed, and any obstructions or hazards in your path. This requires you to be constantly glancing in three directions: ahead at the boat's path, at the speedometer, and at the skier. It is the driver's courtesy and concentration that will make the skier's job as easy as possible.

In order to provide optimum practice conditions for the skier, five responsibilities of the driver should be constantly followed: 1) to provide proper line-up and acceleration: 2) to find and hold the desired speed: 3) to drive in a straight line: 4) to return quickly to a fallen skier: 5) to keep boat wakes in the course to a minimum.

When preparing to pull a barefooter on a start method, line the boat and the skier up in a straight path. If the skier is not directly behind you when taking off, he will drift sideways and may hit the wake.

When the skier signals you to begin accelerating, apply throttle slowly, not all at once. This permits you to make any adjustments in steering and it signals the skier just prior to maximum throttle being applied.

The amount of acceleration needed will vary depending on the type of start. However, the general rule is "better too slow than too fast." A slow pull will only try the skier's patience and ability to hold his breath, while too much acceleration will make the start more difficult and dangerous. The "perfect pull" will vary between barefooters. So it is a good idea to talk over the barefooter's preferences before you pull him.

Keep one hand on the throttle at all times for both safety and adjustment of the speed. Resting your forearm on the throttle box or gunwale allows you to use your fingers and wrist (rather than the whole arm) for more precise control of the throttle. In addition to using the speedometer, changes in boat speed can be sensed by a change in engine tone.

Choose a sufficiently long, straight stretch of calm water for your practice course. Steer in a straight line by aiming at an object on a distant shore. It will also help to look back at the wake to see if the boat has traveled a straight line. Whenever the boat is throwing a wake, it should be driven as nearly parallel to the practice course as possible. This will keep the waves moving away from the course.

When a skier falls, chop the throttle immediately. Make a safe, tight turn and return to the skier along the same path the boat just traveled. Returning to the skier quickly saves time and will help maintain his enthusiasm as well as keep him from getting

Keep one hand on the throttle at all times.

Barefooting 121

BOAT DRIVING

chilled. The tighter the turn, the fewer waves will be thrown back into the course. If you will be continuing to pull the skier in the previous direction, bring the boat all the way down to an idle speed before turning around and returning to the skier. This will prevent rollers from being thrown down the course. Also, never "mush" the boat along at a slower speed. This creates stern rollers perpendicular to the boat path that will travel down the course. Either idle slowly or plane the boat off.

Driving With A Boom

When driving a boat equipped with a boom, always be aware of the boom when turning or approaching obstructions and fallen skiers. While underway, be careful not to dip the boom into the water. This can put excessive strain on the boom and will cause the boat to turn suddenly.

When preparing to pull a skier out of the water with the boom, you will find that it is impossible to idle in a straight line. The boom puts so much leverage on the boat that it makes steering ineffective at idle speed. So when the skier is in deepwater preparing for the start, all you can do is keep the slack out of the line. Any pull of the skier will turn the boat out of position.

During this period preparatory to pulling the skier up, you should line up the boat at an angle 30 to 45 degrees away from the direction you want to go. For example, if you desire a course due north, and the boom is on the left side of the boat, begin takeoff aimed northeast. The pull of the skier planing off will turn the boat left into your desired northerly course. Once underway, the steering of the boat will be more effective.

It is safest not to use a line on the boom that is long enough to reach into the boat. Sometimes the water will sling a dangling handle into the boat hard enough to cause damage or injury. Also a long line will allow the skier to swing dangerously close to the boat.

122 Barefooting

Barefooting 123

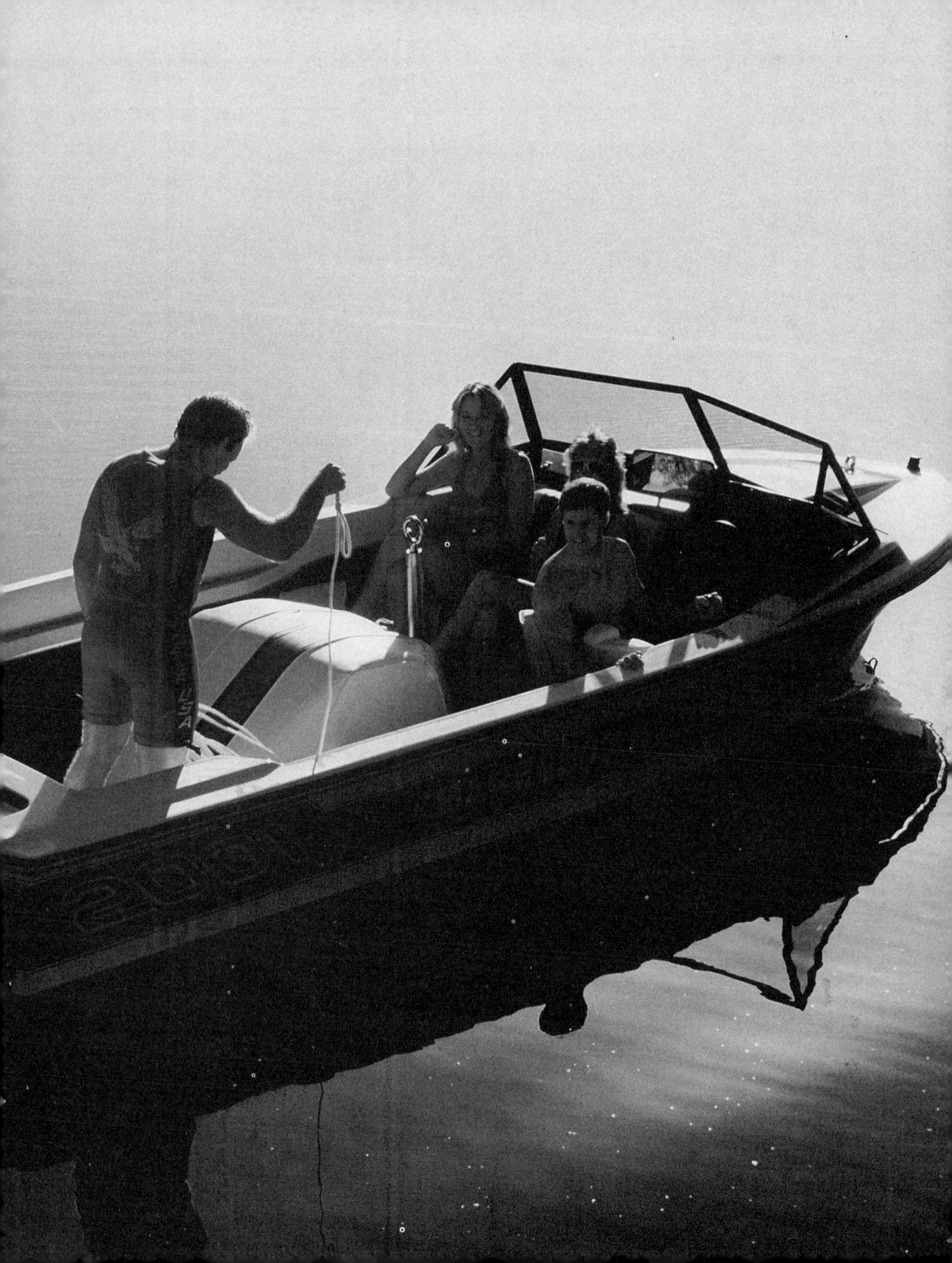

PRACTICE

The key to improving your barefooting skills is getting on the water to practice. However, barefooting is strenuous, and it is possible to wear yourself down physically. Eventually the fatigue becomes a limiting factor which restricts the maximum amount of time you can practice. You should never exceed five to six consecutive days of intensive practice. Always allow one or two days off for your body to rest.

It would be nice if fatigue was the only limiting factor. Realistically though, most of us are limited in our practice by other priorities, such as family, work, school, etc. Determining what to practice in this limited amount of time depends on what your barefooting goals are. For instance, developing consistency will take repeated practice of a specific trick at the sacrifice of spending time learning new tricks. If you are neither a tournament nor show barefooter, consistency may not be important to you. Therefore you can spend your time learning new tricks.

Attitude

Whatever you are attempting, approach it relaxed and confident that you can make it. Eliminate any prejudice about its difficulty, and do not put a time limit on how long you think it will take you to learn. The harder you think it is, the more difficult it will be for you and the less likely you will persistently try it. Before you attempt anything, visualize yourself doing it. Going through the motions of the trick on land will give you a feel for it and an idea of the body motions and positions required. You will be amazed at how quickly you can learn new tricks if you constantly try them with this attitude.

In addition to this positive approach, learn to analyze each attempt, whether successful or not. Ask yourself questions like, "why did I fall?" or, "what did I do that enabled me to make it?" Be aware of your body position and movements. This is where a keen observer is valuable in helping to spot your movements. The observer does not need to be an experienced barefooter as long as you tell him or her what to look for, i.e. "Is the handle into my body?", "Are my knees bent?" The ultimate aid is to have a video tape recorder to play back a practice run in slow motion.

Be careful not to become overly critical of every body movement. Limit your analysis to the basics (leaning away from the boat too much or not enough, handle in, etc.). Although there are times for disciplining your body movements, you should strive to make your movements as natural as possible.

Some mistakes and falls are just poor attempts caused by unfavorable conditions or lack of practice. These will generally disappear and need not be analyzed unless they persist.

Once you learn a new trick, it usually takes a while before you can perform it consistently. During this period continue to concentrate on executing the trick properly. If you start to loose your level of consistency, stop and evaluate the problem before you develop any bad habits. After performing the trick properly a number of times the motion will become an unconscious "muscle memory" reflex.

Champion barefooters are not made in one day. It takes patience and persistence. Do not get angry when you ski poorly. It merely takes the enjoyment out of the sport for you and the boat crew, as well as making practice less productive. No matter how important barefooting is to you, do not vent your frustrations on others. Being able to keep a steady temperament during times of frustration is a mark of maturity. Whether you ski well or poorly, you can still have a good time doing it by maintaining a sense of humor. In all of life, attitude makes the difference.

Barefooting 125

PRACTICE

Practice Sessions For Competitors

Generally, several short sessions bring better results than one or two long sessions. This will keep you mentally and physically fresh, and will provide time for you to analyze your practice between sessions.

Organize your practice. Do not float around trying this, that, and the other. Pick one or two things to devote your concentration to during each session. Make a list of tricks to practice when the water is rough and tricks to practice when the water is calm. Do not restrict your practice to only when the water is perfect. Take advantage of skiing in less than ideal conditions This will help prepare you for adverse water conditions in competition.

If you begin to get in a slump on a particular trick (and everyone does, no matter how long they have been doing it), do not drill it into the ground. Let it sit for a few days and return to the trick with a renewed freshness.

Use the same driver as much as possible. Having someone who knows your speeds and habits can save time and make your practice much more efficient for the time on the water.

Finally, performing for the boat crew is generally unproductive practice. It is best to keep distracting people out of the boat. They can also prevent the driver from concentrating on his responsibilities.

Physical Conditioning

As in many athletic sports, barefooting involves falls which sometimes result in strained or pulled muscles and ligaments. This risk is inherent with the sport. However, injuries can be minimized by being cautious and using common sense, but also by increasing your flexibility and strength. The weaker your muscles and the less flexible you are, the more prone you are to injury.

Everyone is different and has different needs. It is the person who is out-of-shape and barefoots only occasionally that needs a strength training program the most. If you ski frequently, you might reduce your workouts and emphasize mostly stretching. What type and degree of conditioning you need is a personal decision.

Without a doubt, barefooting requires a good deal of strength. The stronger you are, the easier the sport will be to you and the longer you can practice before tiring. The object of strength train-

DO NOT VENT YOUR FRUSTRATIONS ON OTHERS.

126 Barefooting

ing in injury protection is to increase the strength of the muscles surrounding the joints, helping to ease some of the load on the ligaments during a sudden strain. Also, the muscles themselves will be stronger and less likely injured.

Stretching

Stretching should be done year round, three to five days a week, and before barefooting. Once again, different people need to emphasize different parts of the body. For barefooters in general, I recommend that the following area be stretched:

1. Neck — the muscles most commonly strained during barefooting falls.

2. Shoulders — tumbleturns and hanging onto the rope during a fall can often injure an inflexible shoulder.

3. Lower back and sides.

4. Hamstring and groin.

When stretching be sure to stretch slowly to your comfortable limit without bouncing. (Bouncing may actually injure the muscle). Hold the stretched position for five to 10 seconds, and repeat three to five times.

Physical conditioning is something that most people do not enjoy doing. Therefore, it requires a great deal of discipline, but the results will be well worth it. One damaged ligament can keep you off the water for six weeks or more.

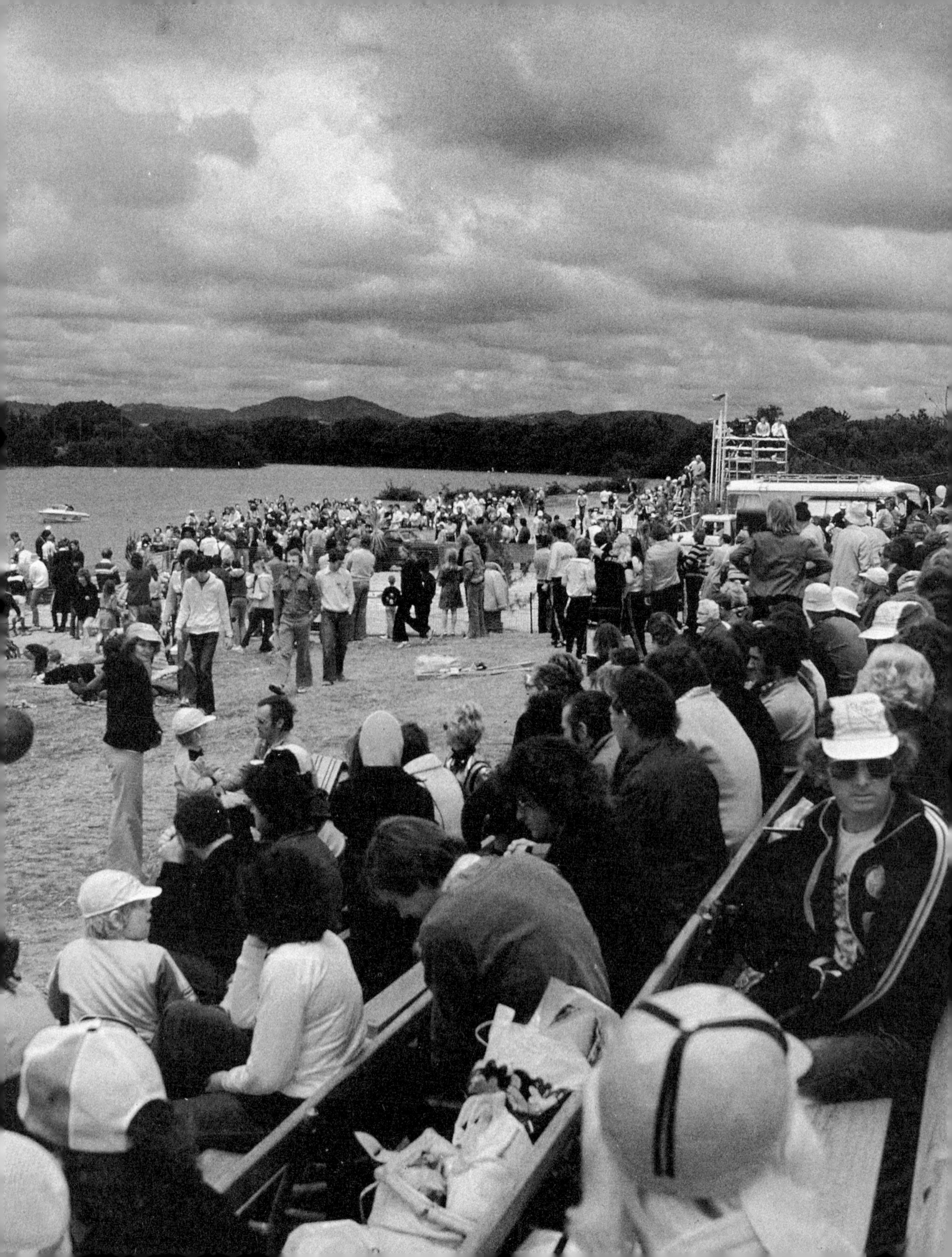

COMPETITION

Competition has been the driving force that has rapidly increased the quality and quantity of barefooters as well as organizing the sport world wide. It provides incentive for participants to better their skills, and most of all gathers footers together to share their enthusiasm and zeal. Of course there are some who compete only for shiny medals, but the majority compete for fun and a source of personal satisfaction. For more information on barefoot tournaments write: American Barefoot Club, P.O. Box 191, Winter Haven, Florida 33880.

Preparing For A Tournament

As a tournament barefooter you need to establish clear goals in advance of the competition. For example, your goal may be to win a specific event, in which case practicing other events is unimportant. On the other hand, an overall competitor may have to sacrifice excellence in an individual event in order to have respectable scores in all events. Each individual must determine what he or she wants to achieve and organize the practice time accordingly.

It is a general rule of thumb to be 80 percent consistent (successful 8 out of 10 attempts) in practice on anything you plan on making in competition. Sometimes obtaining your goal may require you to risk attempting something higher scoring but less consistent. However, the competitor who repeatedly risks "sticking his neck out" will more often then not remain seated when the awards are given out. Don't make it a habit to count on luck!

To perform to your full potential, you need to be rested and strong the day of competition. Therefore, your practices the few days prior to the tournament should be light practices, consisting only of the runs and starts you will be doing in the tournament. At this point it is too late to learn something new and expect to have it consistent for competition.

Practice the day before the tournament should be kept to a minimum. Schedule your travel time to the site so that you will be able to get a good night's

The author competing in the 1980 World Championships in San Francisco.

The site of the first World Barefoot Championships in Canberra, Australia, during 1978.

COMPETITION

sleep. Generally, tournaments start early in the morning. Being physically and mentally tired will decrease your coordination, confidence, and aggressiveness.

Diet

Many people overemphasize diet. A well-balanced diet will undoubtedly be better for you than constant junk food. However, the most important time to watch what you eat is the 24 hours prior to and during the competition. Avoid food that could cause indigestion and uncomfortable gas pains. It is natural for the body to slow down when digesting its food, dulling the reflexes and sense of balance. So the last meal before you ski should be at least two hours beforehand. Avoid any kind of stuffy feeling from eating too much.

If you become hungry within an hour of when you will be skiing, a light snack of fruit juice or fruit high in carbohydrates will provide energy without filling you up.

A trip to the restroom before skiing will help prevent the discomforts of a full bladder or intestine.

At The Site

Once you arrive at the site, check in at the registration area and find out when you will be skiing. You will need to be on hand and ready to ski well before this time in case the tournament progresses faster than expected. They will not stop the tournament for you if you are not there when it is your turn to ski. Arriving late to the starting dock and having to rush onto the water is the second worst thing you can do for your performance. The first is missing your turn altogether.

Do not neglect proper care of your body, particularly your all-important feet! Walking around barefoot at an unfamiliar site is asking for trouble. All it takes is a small cut, bruise, or sticker to cause distracting pain on the water. Also, waiting around all day in the hot sun can really drain your energy. Likewise, on a cold day keep bundled up and warm until your time to ski so you will not be chilled as easily when you take to the water.

A brief warm-up session prior to skiing will help prevent injury and increase your agility. Include some stretching and enough exercise to increase

DON'T GIVE LONG AND CONFUSING INSTRUCTIONS TO THE DRIVER.

your cardiovascular circulation without causing fatigue.

Study the skiing course to see if there is adequate room to prepare for the run or if the boat makes any unusual pattern. Note any point where waves might occur or where the boat path may be close to any obstructions. Most likely, you will not be the first skier in your event, giving you an opportunity to observe the boat path. Visualize yourself on the water going through the entire performance from saying "hit it" to letting go of the rope. Your responsibility is to know what is going to take place before it happens. Don't be surprised!

One of the most important responsibilities is to clearly and concisely communicate your instructions to the driver. You should arrange your skiing to make it as easy as possible for the driver, reducing your dependence on him. Avoid instructions like these: I'll turn around on the ski at 25 m.p.h., plant my foot at 28 m.p.h., step-off at 35 m.p.h., and then up to 40 for the pass." This will only make the driver's job considerably harder and increase the possibility of an improper pull. For the most consistent pulls, learn to plant, step-off, and do your entire run all at the same speed. For start methods, simplify the driver's responsibility as much as possible. For example, "moderate acceleration up to 38 m.p.h." is pretty simple and easy to provide.

Attitude

Your attitude in competition (as well as in all of life) should be that of a sportsman. Webster's Dictionary defines sportsman this way: "a person who can take loss or defeat without complaint, or victory without gloating, and who treats his opponents with fairness, generosity, courtesy, etc."

You shouldn't think more highly of yourself than you ought to think. Be positive, confident, and practiced-up, but recognize that you may still fail. Don't let your pride or ego cause you to fear that. A fear of failure is what causes nervousness. And nervousness can devastate your performance. Maintaining a humble attitude will help provide you with an inner peace and calmness which allows you to perform to your best, as well as enjoy the weekend!

Determine before you take to the water that if you perform poorly you will not let it spoil your day. Recognize that your character will be demonstrated by how you respond to your performance, and that a proven character is more important than a trophy or title. A title only lasts for a short time, but your character will be with you your entire life. It is a mark of maturity to keep a steady temperament during frustrating experiences. Make a decision not to blame anything or anyone should you ski poorly. After all, you probably wouldn't blame them if you skied great!

After winning the World Championships, Mike Seipel stated that it was his attitude which enabled him to win. He had lost the two previous National Championships and several other major tournaments. He said, "Those loses were a result of putting too much pressure on myself to meet the expectations of others. It made me a nervous wreck. Going into the Worlds I relaxed and determined to just ski the best I can and not worry about it. That made all the difference!"

Tournament competition is great fun, and you don't need to be a champion to enter. Many skiers are hesitant to enter because their pride won't allow them to place in the lower ranks. Forget your pride and enter just to learn. It takes tournament experience to become a top tournament barefooter.

Not everyone can become a world-class competitor, but even local competitors receive many of the same benefits. The challenges, the friends, the competition, the victories and the defeats all aid in enriching our lives and building our character. Unfortunately some people put the silver and gold above all else. This can result in many titles, one of which is a bad name. Proverbs 22:1 says, "A good name is to be desired more than riches; favor is better than silver and gold."

So to gain the full enjoyment of competition, seek first to be a sportsman and second to be a champion.

Appendix

Trick Point Values

TRICK	SURFACE 2 Feet	SURFACE 1 Foot	WAKE 2 Feet	WAKE 1 Foot
Somersault	500		650	
Surface Jump off feet	30			
Wake Jump off feet out of or into the wake			40	
Rope on Neck	30	60		
Rope in Teeth	30	60		
Tumbleturn 360	70	100		
Tumbleturn 180	70	100		
One Foot	–	10		
One Foot Backwards		90		
Rope on Foot	–	80		
Rope on Foot Backwards	–	130		
180 turn B – F	120	200	180	260
180 turn F – B	160	220	240	320
360 turn F – F	300	440	450	530
360 turn B – B	380	480		
540 turn B – F	450	630		
540 turn F – B	500	680		
720 turn F – F	600	800		
720 turn B – B	680	860		
180 stepover B – F	150	–	220	–
180 stepover F – B	190	–	280	–
180 rope on foot B – F	–	280	–	420
180 rope on foot F – B	–	250	–	370

Start Methods Point Values

	2 Feet	1 Foot
Group 1. Beach or Deepwater Forwards	40	80
Group 2. Rope on Foot Backwards		300
Group 3. Tumbleturn Forwards	70	100
Group 4. Beach or Deepwater Backwards	140	300
Group 5. Rope on Foot Backwards		250
Group 6. Tumbleturn Backwards	180	340
For a flying start add 30 points.		

132 Barefooting

Glossary

ABC- American Barefoot Club. Organization within the American Water Ski Association governing barefoot competition. P.O. Box 191, Winter Haven, FL 33880 (813) 324-4341.

AXIS- An imaginary line through the shoulders, hips, and feet on which a turnaround is rotated.

BACKWASH- Rolling waves that result from boat wakes hitting and rebounding of stationary objects such as sea walls, piers, boats, etc.

BAREFOOT POSITION- Described in the rules as the position in which barefooter must have possession of the towline and be supported entirely by his barefeet or foot.

BASIC TRICK- The trick preceeding a reverse trick.

BEACH START- Start method initiated by sliding down a beach.

BEAR TRAP- A toehold strap that closes on the foot.

BEAT-AND-SLAM- The trial-and-error method of learning as related to barefooting.

BOG- To sink deeper into the water usually due to slow speed.

BRIDLE- V-shaped rope attached to the handle.

CHOP- Waves created by wind.

CLASSICAL SKIING- Skiing with skis.

CONSISTENCY- Usually expressed as the percent of successful attempts out of total number attempts at a particular maneuver.

CROSS GRIP- Baseball type grip with palms facing opposite directions.

CUTTING- Placing foot or feet on edge and leaning away from the pull of the boat.

DEEP V- Boat bottom design with V-shape. Provides good wake for barefooting.

EDGING- See cutting.

ENDURANCE COMPETITION- Competition to stay on your feet the longest.

FEET-TO-FEET- A trick or jump executed with your weight supported only by your feet, without sitting or laying on the water.

FLATBOTTOM- Boat bottom that is flat. Not desirable for barefooting.

FLYING START- Start Method initiated by attaining an airborne position from a dock or beach.

GLASS- Perfectly smooth water resembling glass. The barerfooters dream.

HIT IT- Verbal command signaling driver to begin accelerating.

HULL- Outer shell of boat.

I/O- Inboard/outboard powered boat. Inboard engine with an attaching outdrive outside the boat.

INBOARD- Boat with the engine inside the boat.

KNEEBOARD- Small surfboard-like sled used as a learning aid for barefooting.

MASTERBOARD- Jump meter control board where jump distances are computed.

Barefooting

GLOSSARY

METER STATIONS- Stationary stands from which the angles of jump landings are sighted.

NORMAL BAREFOOT SPEED- A moderate speed comfortable for barefooting on two feet.

OBSERVER- Extra person in the towboat used to help in skier communications and skier assistance.

ONE FOOT SPEED- Speed necessary to support barefooter's weight on one foot.

ONE FOOT START- Start method completed on one foot only.

OUTBOARD- Boat with engine as a separate unit attached to transom.

PACE- Tempo or rate at which tricks or wake crossings are performed.

PLANE- To skim over the surface of the water.

PLANE-OFF- To accelerate until skimming over the surface of the water.

POLYPROPYLENE- Synthetic plastic composition line with high stretch not desirable for barefooting.

PROPWASH- Turbulence in the center of the lake created by the propeller.

PYLON- Ski rope towing hitch, usually positioned near the center of the boat.

QUICK RELEASE- Device used in the boat to release the rope from the boat.

RATINGS- Levels of achievement used in grading the progression of a skier's performance. Ratings are 1st Class, Expert, and Master.

RERIDE- In competition, where a skier reskis a pass.

REVERSE- A trick performed in the opposite direction or on the opposite foot of the basic trick.

RIDE-OUT-BUOY- In jumping, buoy at which the contestant must barefoot past to receive credit for the jump.

ROLLERS- Rough water usually caused by boat waves.

SEMI-V- Boat bottom with a moderate V-shape.

SPREADER BAR- Bar placed in bridle to open towstrap wide.

STAND-UP BUOY- In jumping, buoy by which the contestant must have regained barefoot position.

STEP-OVER- Trick in which the skier steps over the line with the free foot while turning 180 degrees.

STERN DRIVE- See I/O.

STRETCHED-OUT- Off-balance position with arms and upper body stretched toward boat.

THREE-EVENT SKIING- Competitive water skiing consisting of slaloming through a course, trick skiing, and jumping.

THROW- Turning or forcing a trick excessively hard.

TOE START- Start method in which the rope is held with the foot.

TOESTRAP- Canvas, leather, or nylon strap attached to the rope enabling the skier to hold the rope with the foot.

TOE TRICK- Trick in which the rope is held with the foot.

TORSO- The trunk of the human body.

TRICK RUN- Series of tricks performed in competition.

TRIM- Adjusting the attitude of a planing boat by changing the angle of the engine (outboard) outdrive (I/O), or trim tab (inboard).

TUCK- Drawing your arms and legs in close, curling up the body during a fall.

TURBULENCE- See propwash.

UNWEIGHT- To lessen the weight on one's feet or foot by springing upward.

WAKE- Wave and turbulence created by a moving boat.

WAKE TRICK- Trick executed by jumping off the wake.

WATERTIGHT SHORTS- Shorts usually made of rubber, used to prevent water from being forced up the posterior.

WETSUIT- Neoprene rubber suit. Specially designed wetsuits are used to provide padding, protection, and flotation for barefooter.

WWSU- World Water Ski Union. Governing body of the World Championships.

Mike Botti doing the one ski front-to-back jump out.

Barefooting **135**

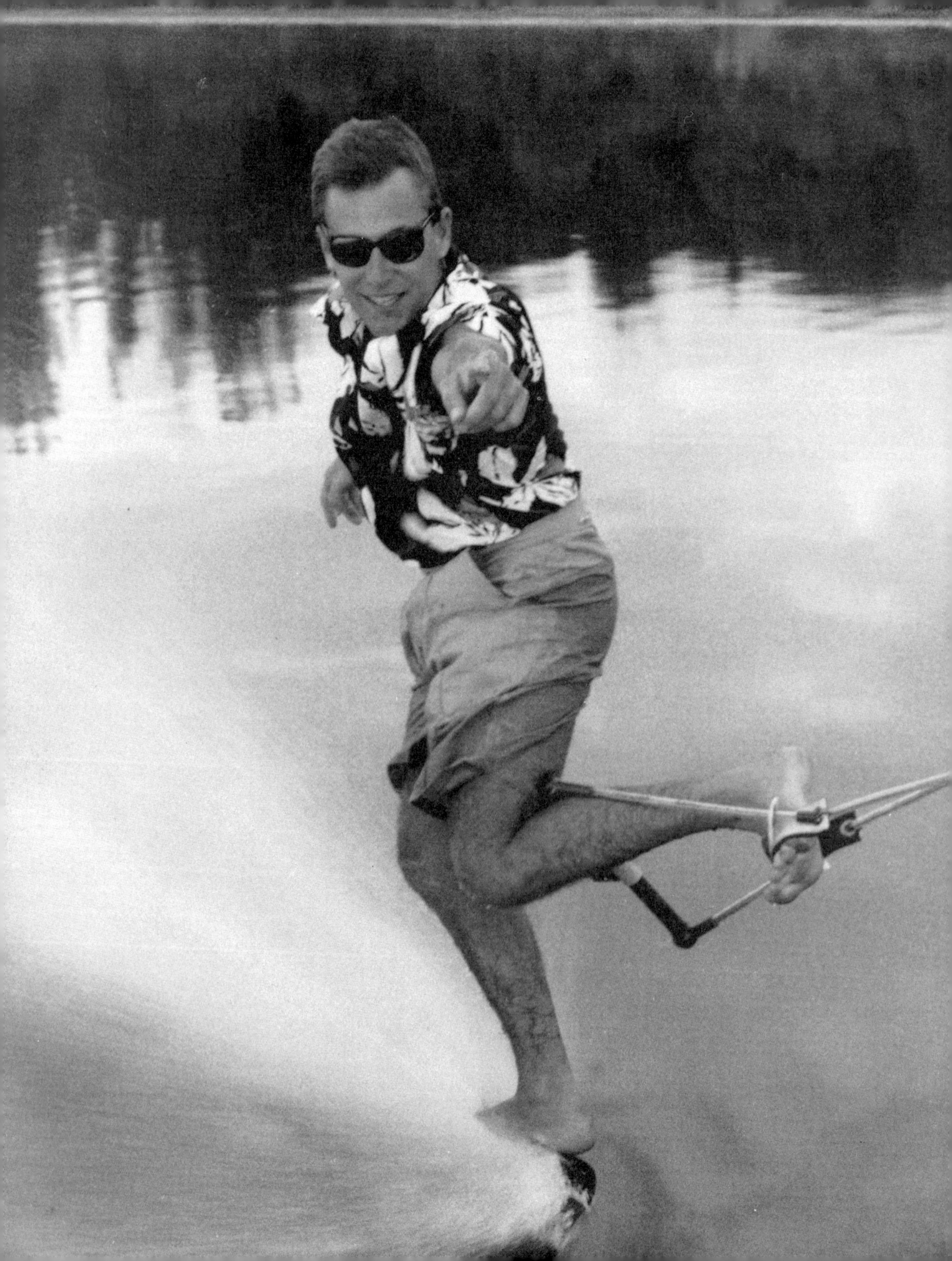

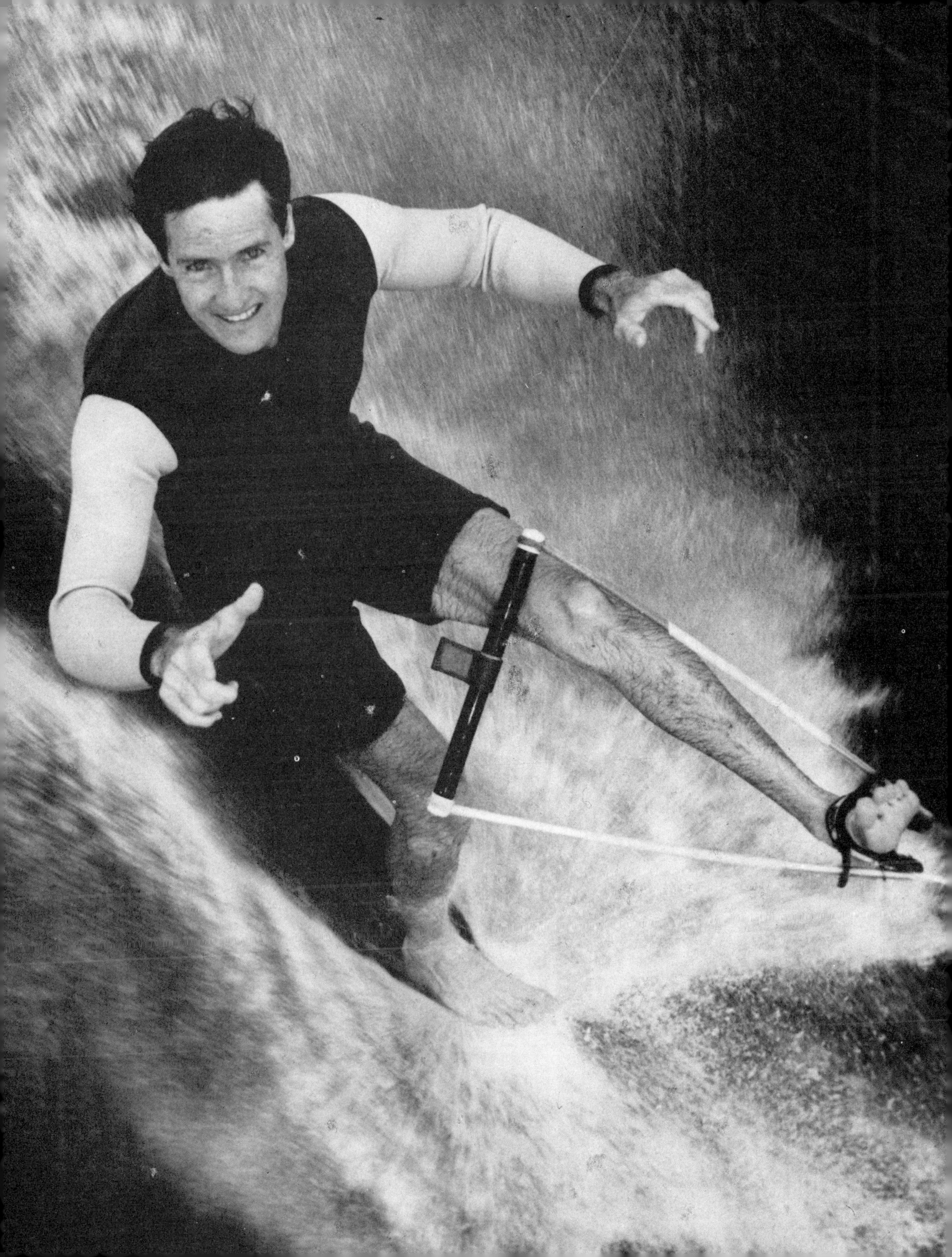

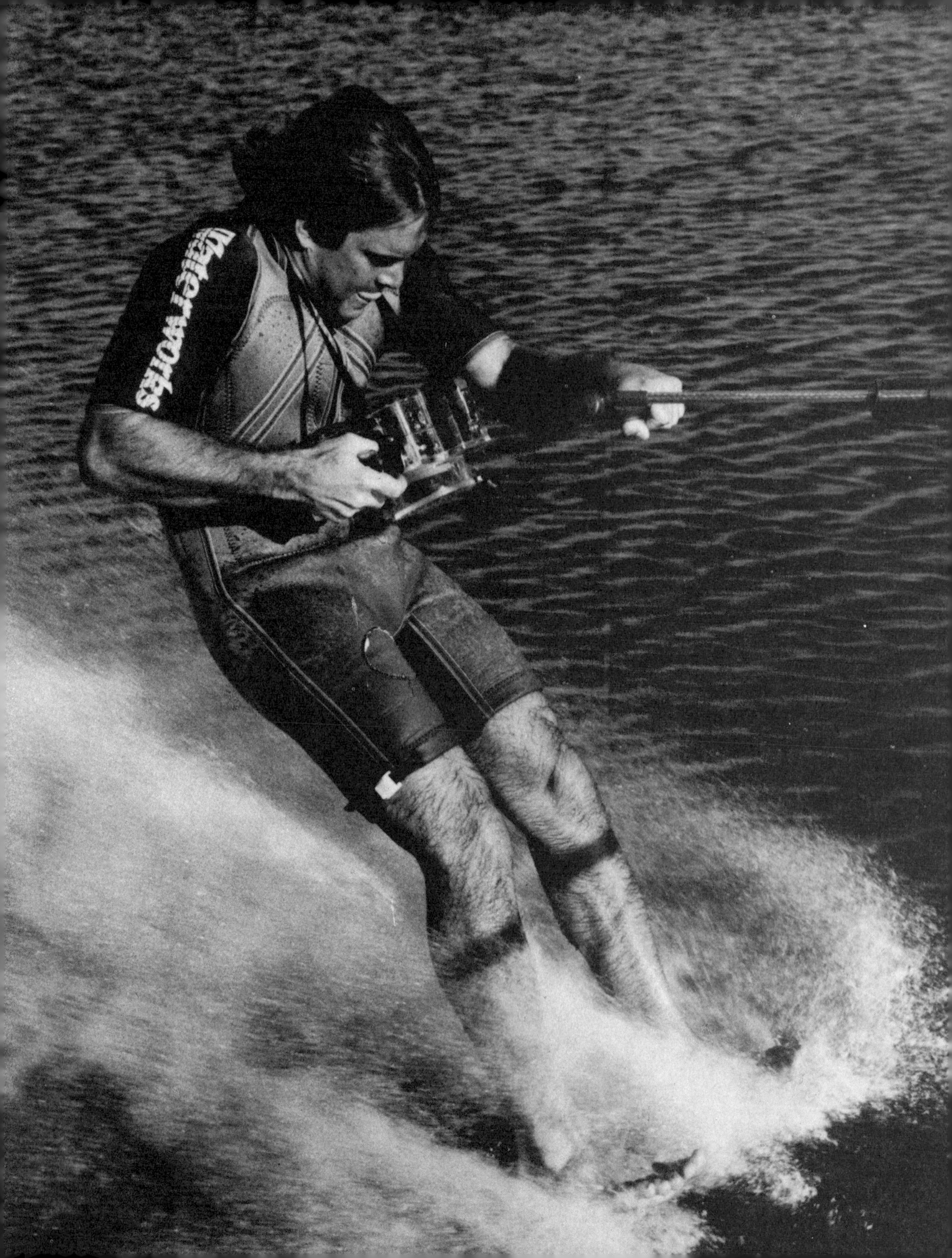

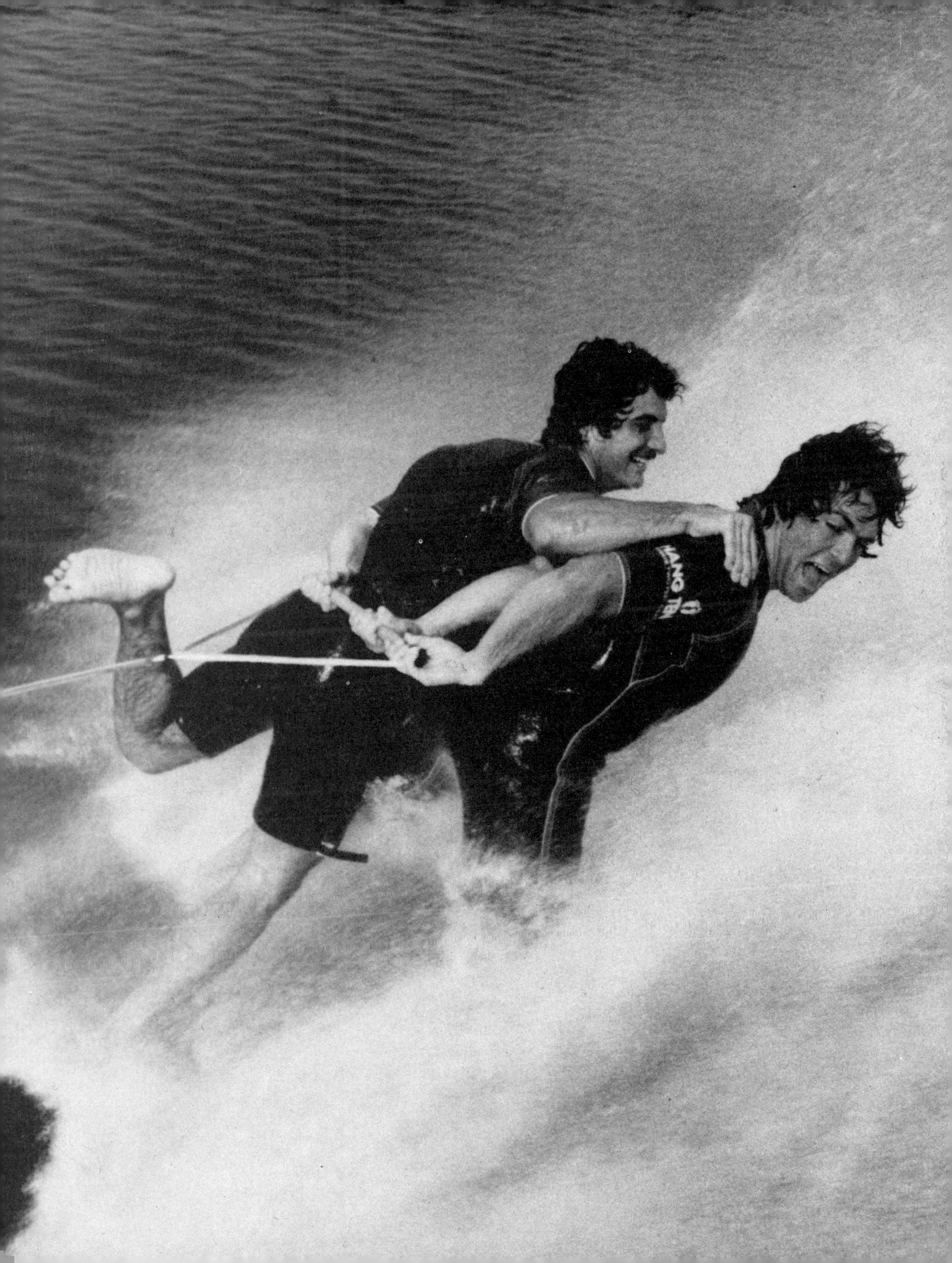
HANG TEN

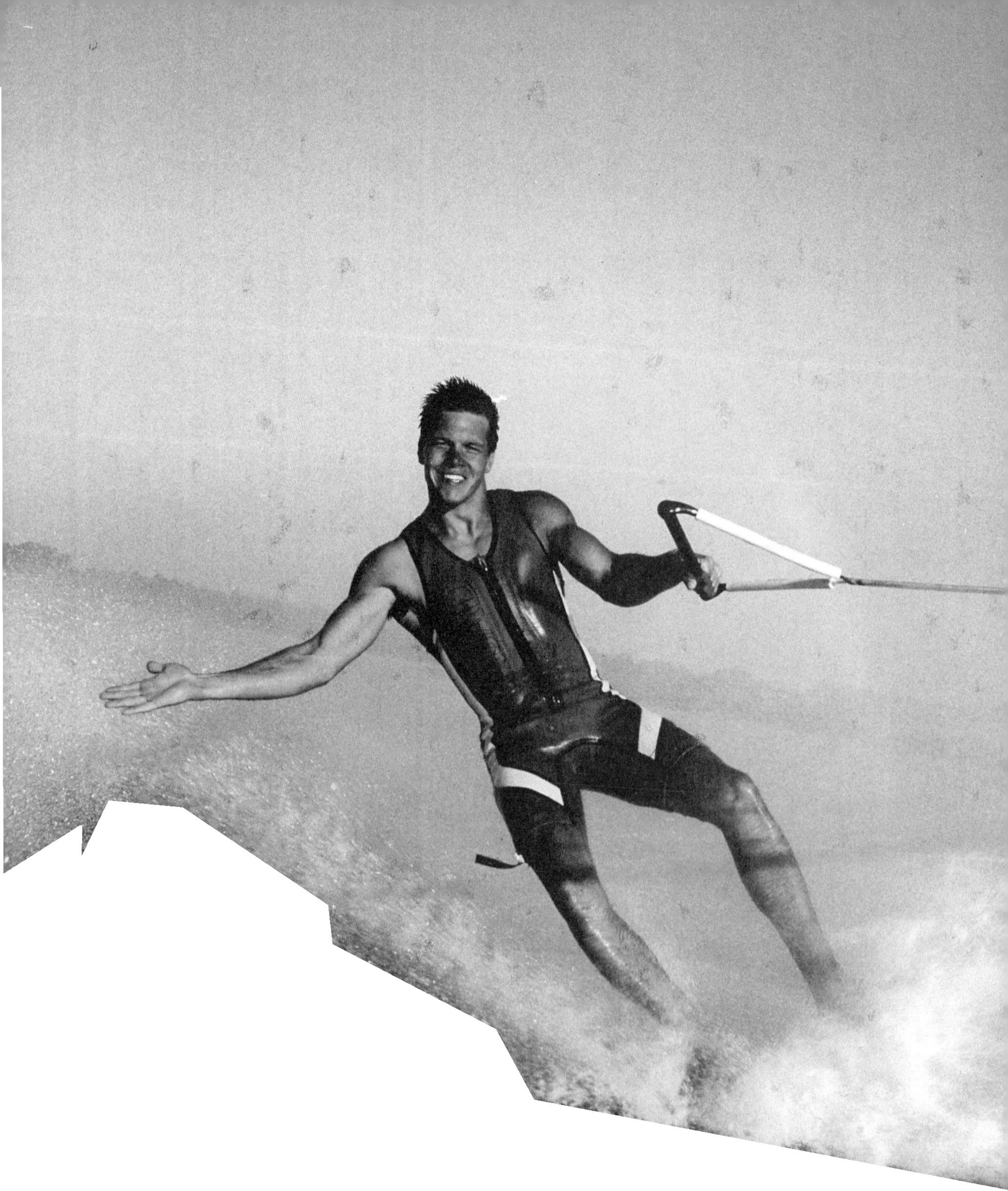

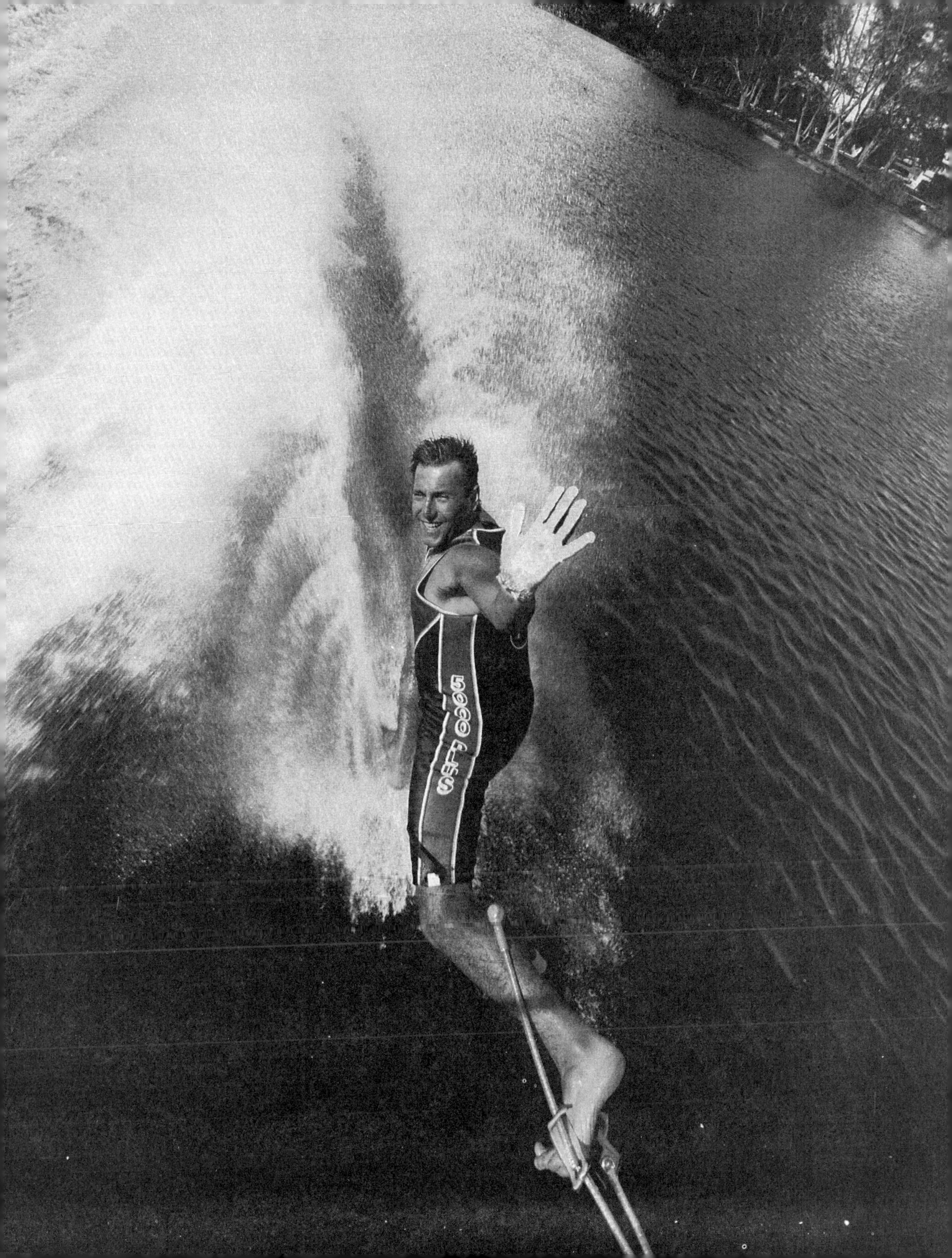
5000

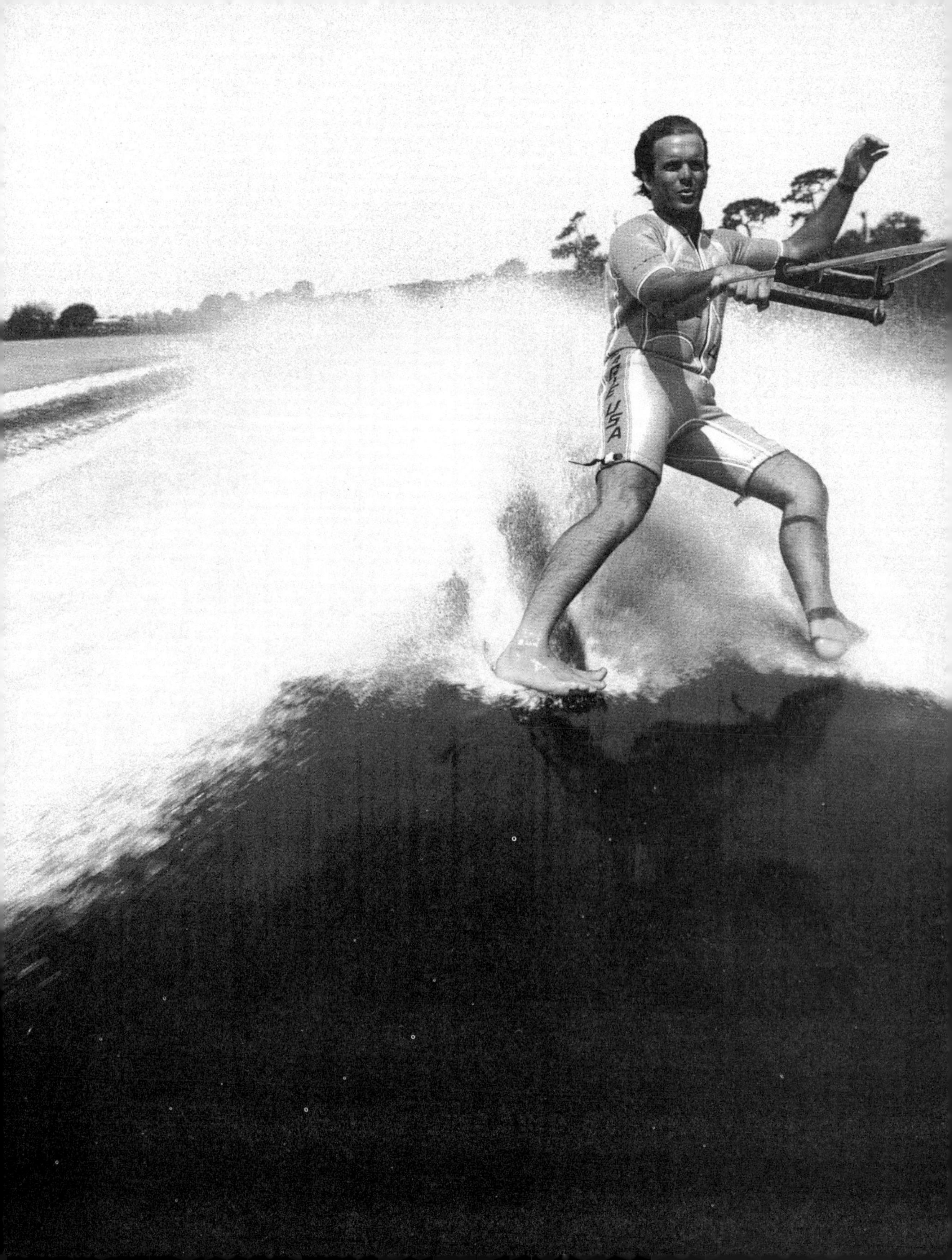
USA